I.V. LOUNGE NIGHTS

Tightrope Books . 2008 . **Toronto**

IV

LOUNGE NIGHTS

Edited by
Alex Boyd & **Myna Wallin**

Tightrope Books
17 Greyton Crescent
Toronto, Ontario
Canada M6E 2G1
www.tightropebooks.com

Canada Council   Conseil des Arts
for the Arts   du Canada

ONTARIO ARTS COUNCIL
CONSEIL DES ARTS DE L'ONTARIO

EDITORS: Alex Boyd & Myna Wallin
COVER PHOTO: Spencer Saunders
COVER DESIGN: Spencer Saunders
TYPESETTING: Carleton Wilson

torontdartsbouncil
An arm's length body of the City of Toronto

Produced with the support of the Canada Council for the Arts, the
Ontario Arts Council and the City of Toronto through the Toronto
Arts Council.

PRINTED AND BOUND IN CANADA

LIBRARY AND ARCHIVES CANADA CATALOGUING IN PUBLICATION

I.V. Lounge nights / edited by Myna Wallin, Alex Boyd.
Anthology celebrating the 10th anniversary of the I.V. Lounge
reading series.

ISBN 978-0-9783351-4-4

1. Canadian fiction (English) – 21st century. 2. Canadian poetry
(English) – 21st century. I. Wallin, Myna II. Boyd, Alex

PS8251.I823 2008   C810.8'006   C2008-901595-9

For Kevin,
with thanks for ten years.

Contents

Introduction

THERE SHOULD BE some kind of special literary award for spending five years getting tense every time someone creaks across wooden floors in the middle of a reading. Perhaps just a wooden plank nailed to a base.

Started in 1998 by Paul Vermeersch, and handed to me on the fifth anniversary in 2003, the I.V. Lounge Reading Series has been a pleasure – occasionally creaking or not – and as the series passes the ten year mark, it's interesting to note that it has never changed, because there's no need to fix what isn't broken. The format is simple: three readers who keep to about fifteen or twenty minutes, and breaks between the readers, because literature shouldn't be an endurance test (and we can all probably agree literature is somewhat marginalized these days, which makes it even more critical). There's a mix of poetry and fiction, as well as new and established writers to bring in a mixed audience, and an audience that gets exposed to someone or something they might not have checked out otherwise, and finally no charge at the door and no open stage. Again, I think it goes back to creating an accessible, professional, enjoyable evening for a more marginalized art form, and declining to have an open stage isn't elitist, any more than editing a magazine and declining random pages is elitist. It never hurts to have an incredibly comfortable place to host the readings, with "lounge" in the name to suggest the comfortable oasis the series has become.

The series is run without grants, but readers planning a tour or passing through town have been booked whenever possible, and this anthology has representatives from Vancouver, Ottawa, Montreal and Fredericton. Finally, though tooting my own horn has probably given way to blasting my own horn, I've made efforts to book the occasional spoken word artist or overtly experimental writer, even though it isn't my usual cup of tea. The word "occasional" may not sound like much, but the different camps are often utterly segregated.

My sincere thanks to anyone who has ever volunteered time to read for the warmth of the experience, the drink tickets and the notion a few books might be sold. Many thanks to Paul Vermeersch for starting the series, and showing how it's done. My thanks to Myna Wallin for being a kind, thoughtful, diplomatic and sharp-eyed co-editor on this anthology, I've learned first-hand that it's a lot more work than you'd expect. My thanks to manager Kevin Jones, to Myna Wallin for guest-hosting the series at times, and to Halli at Tightrope Books for publishing this anthology as a tremendous souvenir from the tenth year of the series, as well as a snapshot of a vibrant Canadian literary culture – not a snapshot of someone droning on in a lecture hall, but someone chatting comfortably, preparing to engage an audience, ordering a martini and catching sight, ever so briefly, of Quincy the cat.

Alex Boyd
TORONTO • 2008

I.V. LOUNGE NIGHTS

Steve McOrmond

THE END OF THE WORLD

The persistent cough, the routine procedure,
the congenital defect, the faulty wiring,
the fire in the starboard engine, the *force majeure*,
the mistress in the city, the last spirited thrust,
the little breeze off the coast of Africa,
the apples torn from the trees,
the unopened mail, the paperboy ringing the bell,
the atmospheric anomaly, the snow on the TV,
the hot wind with its tincture of rotting fish,
the wasps-nest of tumors, the drug-resistant strain,
the feeding tube, the shunt, the morphine drip,
the fatigue and general malaise,
the night inventory of the medicine cabinet,
the sleeping pills, the razor blades,
the reversals suffered as a child,
the bend in the road, the patch of black ice,
the telephone pole advancing in the high beams,
the statistical improbability, the cougar attack,
the stray piece of cosmic debris, the locals celebrating
the wedding of the loveliest girl in the village
by firing their guns into the air.

DONUT SHOP

It's the hole that fascinates. So many customers
buying what isn't there. *Drive through, please.*

The construction worker is up before dawn,
hard hat, steel toes. The office tower climbs

another storey. The butcher drags his carcass
out of bed, sharpens knives, grinds hamburger.

The drugstore clerk, stocking shelves, looks away
as the woman sweeps jars of baby food into her purse.

In the shower, the bank teller sings, clambering
up the octaves. A slender boy opens an account

with rolls of dimes. On a warbly upright piano,
the student hammers out something resembling a tune.

She works hard at her lessons and she is learning slowly.
The world isn't so much without us.

Alexandra Leggat

KID AIRPLANE

GEM STARES AT the traffic light. Wipes her sweating forehead with her shirtsleeve as the light turns green, yellow, red, green, yellow, red, green. Her heart thumps. She checks her watch. She's meeting a man who hits people for a living. The photos she's been studying show a large nose, broken more than a hundred times, swollen, disfigured. She makes her way into the coffee shop, orders a black coffee and sits at a table in the corner. Every man that walks through the door has a large nose and scans the room like they are looking for someone. In her purse, Gem carries a travel-size bottle of Grand Marnier, pours a drop of the orange liquid into her coffee cup resting on her lap beneath the table. She figures that he will smell the booze on her breath mixed with the bitterness of coffee but if he fails to like her for who she is, fuck him.

A stocky, tanned man with a smile on his face approaches the table.

"Gem?" he asks.

She nods, quickly sips the coffee. It blankets the nerves prickling beneath her thin skin, warms her throat.

"You're handsome," she says.

"So are you," he says. He removes his coat.

He's smaller than she imagined; twitches, sniffs. His eyes are steady. He never looks down. Gem thinks that if she were to look under the table his feet would be dancing around under there. Yet the stillness of his upper body defies that notion.

"Are you ever afraid to fight?" she asks.

"No," he says. "It's a mental thing."

"Oh," she says.

"Were you afraid to meet me?" He asks.

She hesitates. A minute ago, she would have been honest, told him "Fuck yeah; I froze at the traffic light, sweat through my new shirt. Contemplated turning around." She smiles, drops her head, tells him, "Of course not."

The stakes have changed. She's happy that he didn't start by asking questions like, where are you from? What do you do? What's your middle name? Do you have siblings? All the questions that she was going to ask him if he'd been reserved or awkward. Without taking his eyes off hers he nods and flicks his neck to the left then to the right. She reaches for her coffee and he withdraws, then relaxes, and she wonders if he always anticipates a punch. He cracks his thick neck. Two young women look at him as they pass and whisper to each other.

Gem sips her coffee. The Grand Marnier loosens her thoughts. He sniffs, stares at her. She tries to avoid his eyes, looks behind her.

"Never look away," he says, flicks the side of his nose with his thumb, jostles in his chair, and laughs.

"Hemingway liked boxing," she says. "You know? The writer."

"And fishing," he says. "I don't like fishing."

"And bullfighting," she adds.

"I have a pit bull," he says.

"Do you make it fight?"

He cocks his head. "That's cruel," he says.

The question or the practice, she thinks to herself but he's sweating a little and gritting his teeth, making his jaw beat.

"Do you like horse racing?" he asks.

Gem's eyes widen. She does, very much. She waves her large hands in the air and tells him that she loves it. He blushes and his shoulders drop. He nods and taps his muscular, nicked fingers on the table, takes a sip of his green tea. The sun streams through the window. His eyes are like marbles, green marbles with brown flecks. They're not empty like some people's eyes.

"Let's go to the track, some day," he says.

"Sure," she says. "Some day."

She wonders if he bets on the ponies or just observes. Then she contemplates his temper, wonders if he has a bad one, if in between bouts, there's a lot of pent up frustration. She thought he'd be taller. She read he was a lightweight, but didn't think lightweight meant short.

"Does it hurt?" she asks

"Only when you get hit in the side."

"Of the head?"

"The body: kidneys, spleen, liver. When you get hit in the head, it's like the lights go out for a second, you don't feel anything."

"Race horses bring me to tears," she says. "They're too beautiful."

"Is there such a thing as too beautiful?" he asks.

She wonders.

"Yes," she says.

A guy in track pants and a blue T-shirt comes up to him and shakes his hand, pats him on the back, then walks away smiling. He's famous, Gem likes that. She asks what she should call him.

"The Kid," he says.

"I know that, but I mean another name?"

"Airplane, Kid Airplane."

He swings his neck to the left, sniffs. She imagines taking him to family gatherings, the look on her father's face when she arrives with the champion lightweight boxer, Kid Airplane. All these years he's been waiting for his daughter to hook up with someone and she hooks up with a star, an athlete. He'd be over the moon. Her sisters will seethe. Their overweight lawyer husbands will finally take a back seat at the dinner table, the fireplace. Everyone will gather around The Kid asking him to tell them about his greatest fights, the time he was knocked unconscious but came back to win the championship in the fifth round with a broken nose and an eye sealed shut with blood. Her dad will wink at her across the dinner table and flash the thumbs-up and her mother will blush when The Kid tells her how much he loves her peach pie, that he rarely eats pie when in training and he's always in training.

Gem finishes her coffee. Fluffs up her hair, looks around to see if anyone else has noticed that The Kid's out with a lady friend. She wishes she wore her low cut black blouse, pencil skirt and high heels. The Kid watches her. He smiles, almost looks away.

"I'm happy, you know," says Gem. "I'm not here because I need to be."

The Kid swallows, rubs his hands together, and flicks his head from side to side. Gem's feet dance beneath the table. He doesn't feel strange, like she'd just met him.

"You seem pensive," says The Kid. "What are you thinking? Lay it on me. I can take it."

"That I'm a lot taller than you."

"There's nothing we can do about that."

"You're right."

"I used to date a jockey," he says.

"Was she miniscule?"

"No, not in that jockey way, just in a petite female way."

"What's the difference?"

"She didn't look odd."

Gem's stomach falls. She didn't want to go to the races anymore. Why be the tall woman he brings to the track to annoy the tiny successful woman he really wants to be with? So she tells him. His eyes moisten. He leans his elbows on the table and whispers, "While fighting for a space along the rail in the final stretch of a big race her right leg was crushed between horses. She managed to hang on for a few feet then fell off her mount and was pummelled by the other horses. She died." He leaned back against his chair. They just met. Gem doesn't want to hear about his exes.

"Would you have married her?"

"No."

"Why?"

"She was never home."

"Doesn't your career keep you on the road?"

"Not anymore. I just retired."

"No."

He's handsome and she likes being around him, even though he's twitchy and sniffs a lot – retired changes everything. If she brings the retired boxer around for dinner it won't have the same impact. Her sisters will look down their noses at him. Her father will ask, "What the hell is he going to do now?" Then he'll make a clicking noise with his mouth and her mother will roll her eyes and shrug her shoulders. She won't make pie. Gem checks her watch. It's feeding time. The plants need to be watered, the fish fed, the dog walked. She doesn't have time for an unemployed man in her life. She stands up. The Kid stands up.

"I want to walk you home," he says.

She wonders how he knows that she lives close by, walking distance. She looks around the room. Makes eye contact with two women having a coffee. They sneer and look away. Look at me, she says with her eyes, remember what I'm wearing, green jacket, black pants, floral shirt, my hair is short, dirty blonde. I have round gold-rimmed glasses. I'm about 5'8", 130lbs and my ears are not pierced. I have a scar above my top lip from falling against a sharp object when I was young. Remember me, so that when I go missing you can tell the police that you saw me with a short, stocky man with a black jacket, bald and a crooked nose. Tell them you think I left with that lightweight boxer you've seen on TV – Kid Airplane. She can see it now all over the papers, *Local Woman Abducted by Newly Retired Lightweight Champion-Kid Airplane; The Kid Lashes Out; Retired Boxer Loses His Mind; Out of the Ring, The Kid's a Lost Soul; Retirement's Hard on a Professional Athlete.* Her dad would be amazed. Her mother would know exactly how to field the slew of phone calls. Her sisters for the first time would want to tell everyone that they are related to the woman in the paper.

They walk out of the coffee shop and down the road.

"I like you," says The Kid.

"Why?"

He stops, looks at Gem. His face though visibly battered over the years is soft and kind. He tells her that he wants to get into politics. She nods, knows nothing about politics. They continue to walk. His feet are small. She towers over him and it makes her feel strong. He stops again.

"My real name is Neil. You can call me Neil. I want you to know the real me, Neil. I am Neil and you know it feels really good to tell you that. Wow, thanks for sharing the first day of my new life with me."

Gem looks down at the ground, at her tattered shoes. She's glad she didn't wear heels. She senses her dog pacing around the living room, wondering where she is. She's never late, never deviates from the routine. Neil looks around, sniffs. Now she knows his real name, when he sniffs it's like he has an allergy, a cold, a nervous tick. She liked him better when he didn't seem real.

Carmine Starnino

TALE OF THE WEDDING RING

Who'll have me, the wedding ring cried out.
Who'll rescue me now that I'm unwanted?
I, said the earth. I'll hold you like a seam of silver,
hide you inside rock and kiss where it hurts.
Like hell, said the fire. I'll melt down your shape
and forge from it a new life: less workaday,
less fixed, more fluid, no strife. No way, said the water.
I'll wash your mind clean and you'll wake
to a cool, clear-running forgetfulness,
refreshed. Forget it, said the tree. I can play the part.
Try on one of my roots for size, might fit.
Might not, said the bird. Join me in my nest:
days and nights under warm feather
and above the reach of the world, hosting
the whole of my brood. But before it could choose
the moon walked into the weeping O
of the ring's eye, wedged where it had been flung
– still pledging itself, still a trinket of its own
lost cause – and accepted it just as it was.

HEAVENOGRAPHY

Working-class clouds chug west. All day, they blow apart. All day, they bloom back: churning, thick-piled, and already beginning to fray. Up to speed, no tilt, swept from somewhere else to right here, running alongside traffic, but mostly on stand-by, filibustering, giving nothing away, shed shapes of no-shape, shapes parked with the handbrake off and drifting. Working-class clouds are old pros at the god-like point of view, vertigo-free, gaze down at the backs of birds in flight, at pin-head people. Working class clouds sit tight and bull's-eye every new space they hit. Working-class clouds tiptoe neck and neck, pitter pat, at good clip, understudying each other, taking a stab at lookalikeness, becoming clones, or close enough. Working-class clouds eke out their melt, morph on the installment plan, think-twice fleet, vite, and then some. Working-class clouds dig deep, 3pm and still clocking klicks, legging it longwise. Working-class clouds make tracks over the working-class, St. Henri, NDG, Parc-Ex, St. Leonard, Laval, railyards, park-ing-lots and smokestacks, grain silos, bridges and waterways. Working-class clouds take turns taking down directions, try to read back what they wrote, but can't. Working-class clouds are tripping, sensing just how high up they are. Working-class clouds are a thousand tons of rereturned rain freshly painted and set upright to dry. Working-class clouds are breeze-fed flocs, hardly anything, whathaveyous, an idea in trial and error, one-of-a-kind demos. Working-class clouds never hang around longer than they have to but always hold out for bet-ter. Working-class clouds are self-made men, having brung themselves up from street-level, from scratch. Working-class clouds could give a shit, represent nothing more than atmos-pheric farting around, a bunch of good-for-nothings stuck between going and gone. Working-class clouds hold the air in white hands, like babies at suck. Working-class clouds bob this way and that. Working-class clouds touch down safely in the higher precipices, leave appreciable skid marks. Working-class clouds are built in a hurry from random parts: scraps of billow, lengths of bulge. Working-class clouds are beamed in live, a real-time film of floating, sky broadcasting endless eyewitness accounts of itself. Working-class clouds, deadline looming, knuckle under, get to grips with the situation, mutter *here goes* and go hard at it. Working-class clouds are above it all, regard the hydraulics that gives them their height as a right. Working-class clouds don't really know who's running the show. Working-class clouds are what happen when sky works up a full head of steam with nowhere to go. Working-class clouds are uploaded fluorescence, exoskeletal shingles of light, bits of 2-D happenstance our eye is always on. Working-class clouds get a lot of wear and tear. Working-class clouds are the dribs and drabs of a slow leak:*pffft*. Working-class clouds are flat tires slapping the road for mile-on-mile. Working-class clouds are taking on water and soon will singlemindedly bail. Working-class clouds live large, late-Turner doozies that fit flank to flank, close ranks, press-ganged and darkening. For working-class clouds, ill winds are a real buzz kill. Working-class clouds always run out of time, and when that happens we catch the wetness full in the face and sprint from street to park shelter and wait. Working-class clouds, your head in them.

Shaun Smith

FOOL'S GOLD

CURTIS WAS LISTENING to Chip. "I mean, there's no reason you, or I, or even Peggy for that matter, shouldn't be able to have the things we want."

They were sitting at a plastic table on a patio full of noisy university students in downtown Toronto. Curtis, dressed in his usual faded black T-shirt and paint-splattered blue jeans, sat in the shade of a green canvas umbrella, unshaven, sweating, drinking a beer. Chip sipped mineral water and had turned his chair into the sun so he could deepen his already dark tan. Curtis hated the sunlight. Hated it, except to look at it, to sit in the shade and look at whatever was happening in the light. And right now what was happening was Chip: his eyes. For the last few minutes the sun had been shining at an angle that made Chip's irises glow like gold. Chip didn't know it, but last year those irises had been the inspiration for Curtis' giant rondo, *Super Nova*.

Chip shifted his pager on the table; the amber eyes studied the display. "I mean, I don't know if I should stay here or move out to Vancouver, man," he said, shaking out his ponytail and retying it. "Be closer to L.A, you know?"

Curtis nodded.

"I mean, I'm thirty-one now, man. I've lived here all my life. I deserve some comfort, right? Material and emotional?"

"Sure."

"I mean, look at you. How long you been driving that van?"

"Two years September, since Peg and I got married."

"And what's it gotten you?"

Curtis said nothing.

"See? And you're thirty-five."

"Thirty-six."

"I bet you haven't sold a single painting in a year. Oh man, maybe I should just move to L.A."

Curtis sipped his beer. The light was leaving Chip's eyes now. "What about you?"

"Hey, the man's got my one-sheet at this very moment. Tomorrow I could be money." He adjusted his chair, tilted his face up, and closed his eyes.

Curtis' gaze fell on the thick gold hoop that hung from his right ear. "What man?"

Chip dropped the name of a prominent film director from Toronto.

"Great," Curtis said. The hoop dangled above the crisp collar of Chip's tennis shirt, gleaming against his browned skin like something a pirate might wear. Curtis thought: coffee, cinnamon, vanilla, sugar.

"It's called 'The Atoll,'" Chip said, though Curtis hadn't asked. "It's about this tribe of natives in the South Pacific who fight to stop a nuclear test on their island."

Curtis remembered hearing something on the radio about a nuclear experiment in French Polynesia. "That's cool."

Coconut. Wet sand. Salt. Driftwood.

"I should get going," Curtis said, "I gotta pick up some beer for the party tonight." But he was thinking now about the materials he would need – canvas, gesso, linseed, turps, pigments. He was thinking about the colours he would be mixing this time next week, thinking about the stretcher he would have to start building tomorrow, about the space it was going to take. He was thinking about all the work that lay ahead.

When the bill came, Chip didn't even look at it. Ever since university, he never had any money. Curtis paid and they went out to the sidewalk.

"I mean I only want what's coming to me, you know?"

Curtis nodded.

They stood watching traffic.

"Hey, can you spot me twenty, man?"

Curtis took out his wallet.

• • •

CURTIS DROVE SLOWLY down Bathurst Street behind a street-car. The delivery van, which he'd borrowed from the frame shop for the weekend, didn't have air conditioning and it was like a pizza oven. As he maneuvered around the streetcar, he could see tall anvil-shaped clouds rising far to the south above the lake. Even though Peggy wasn't there today, he was headed for the art supply store on Queen West where she worked, and where her coworkers would let him buy things with her staff discount. He would need titanium white, napthol red, burnt sienna, raw umber, cadmium yellow and mars black. Pigments. And canvas, number twelve, 144 inch. And lots of gold leaf. It was going to cost, but that was okay: *Super Nova* was going tomorrow. Curtis and Peggy lived in a warehouse near Richmond and Bathurst and an investment banker on a studio tour had come by last week and bought the big rondo. Cut a cheque right on the spot. It was the first painting Curtis had sold in months. Indeed, in a year. He'd delayed deliver-ing it to the guy's office because he wanted it up for the party tonight. But now he was ready to see it go. He needed the space for his new work: another giant rondo, an enormous gold hoop shining against a tan-and-white background. It would be called *Fool's Gold*.

"A sequel," he said to no one.

• • •

"GAWD IT'S HOT!" Pearl said.

Peggy looked down at the water and tried to ignore her. The surface of Lake Ontario was slick with grime and chemicals. Peggy and Pearl had just come from dim sum at Queen's Quay Terminal and were now standing in the sun at the railing along the quay between the Harbour Castle Hilton and the Toronto Star building. Captain John's Seafood Restaurant, an enormous dead yacht, floated there, moored to a pier at the base of Yonge Street, its bow forever pointing north, bilge forever pumping from a pipe at its stern.

"Filthy," Pearl said, flicking a cigarette at a dead sunfish.

Pearl had flown in from Vancouver that morning to begin a catering job on a film. Peggy thought she might like to go down to the water for lunch, but typical of Lake Ontario in August, the water stank of pollution and Pearl had immediately expressed revulsion. Now, despite herself, gazing down at the water, all Peggy could think about was how beautiful it looked: chemical rainbows in algae-green foam, the sunlight sinking in the murk from pale jade to beryl. She wondered how she might recreate the effect in a glaze.

"I hate ships," Pearl said, looking at Captain John's. "So much of them are under water."

Peggy looked up at the old yacht. Its rusted red-and-white hull reminded her of a series of vases she'd thrown last August, when Pearl was last staying with her and Curtis, working on another film. The red-and-white vases, inspired by a lasagna pan Pearl had left for two days in the sink, had a heavily crackled surface that had been very difficult to achieve. Last August had been just as hot as this one and Pearl had complained endlessly. During the summer, Peggy usually ran her kiln only at night, to keep the heat down. But while Pearl was staying with them, Peggy had to do it when Pearl was at work. So she'd spent her two days off a week last August sweltering in the non air-conditioned loft, windows thrown wide, the sun baking her inside the building like one of her own pots in the kiln. When the two days were done, she would have to wait five more to continue. In an effort to appease, Curtis bought two big oscillating fans from Canadian Tire, but even then Pearl complained. "Jesus, it's hot," she would say each night upon return from the set. "You're not running that bloody clay oven are you?"

All of lunch today had been spent talking about whether or not Pearl should move to Toronto – "they keep flying me back here" – or just move down to Los Angeles. She was writing a screenplay – "catering has its limits, you know" – and apparently she'd had some interest from someone – "a big producer" – at one of the studios. She dropped a name – "he has my treatment at this very moment" – but Peggy had never heard of him. Pearl mentioned a few of his movies – "all blockbusters" – but Peggy hadn't seen any of them. Peggy said she was happy for her and wished Pearl luck. "It's called 'The Atoll,'" Pearl said. "About a band of Indians in the South Pacific who try to stop a nuclear bomb on their island."

Peggy remembered reading a newspaper article about a French atomic experiment. "That's great."

Pearl said she hoped Peggy didn't mind, but she would have to call 'the big producer' when they got back to the loft. She'd forgotten her cell in Vancouver.

Pearl didn't ask about Peggy's ceramics business. It had taken most of last August to perfect the crackle glaze. In the end, she'd made five vases, four of which she sold to a new Italian restaurant that closed ten months later. Her vases went to the liquidator. Since then, she'd not had much luck selling anything. Looking up at the ship's paint-chipped hull now, she was glad she'd kept one of the vases for herself.

"I think it's a nice old ship," Peggy said.

But Pearl wasn't interested in the ship any more. She was playing with her earrings, which looked like little gold twigs, and gazing out over the water towards the islands that enclose

Toronto's harbour to the south. Tall violet clouds loomed in the sky. "Pirates used to bury their gold on desert islands," Pearl said, "and then forget where they'd left it." She made a snorting sound. "I mean, what fucking good could that do? All the guys I meet are just like that: stupid and broke." Ever since high school, Pearl had only dated losers.

"We should get going," Peggy said, "I have to pick up some wine for the party tonight." But she was thinking now about the new vases, about how many sweltering days off it would take to perfect the pollution glaze, about the materials – feldspar, china clay, whiting, flint, copper oxide – she would need, about how much it would all cost, about all the work that lay ahead. And she was thinking about how Pearl would complain endlessly of the heat.

In the liquor store, Pearl finally asked about Peggy's pottery. "Hey, how's that bowl business of yours? Are you still running that clay oven?"

• • •

CHIP ARRIVED JUST after eight-thirty. The windows of the loft were thrown wide. Five stories above the street, the large corner room lay darkened, the humid air being pushed about by two big fans. In the tall south-facing windows, thunderheads mushroomed in the twilight above the lake. A jumbled soup of noises flowed in off the street: traffic, laughter, streetcars, sirens. Only one other guest had arrived.

"Chip, this is Pearl," Peggy said.

Chip set a bottle in a sweaty paper bag on the island in the kitchen and offered his hand across. "Hi."

Pearl was wearing a pale-green sleeveless top and fanning herself with a movie magazine. She raised her hand to his as though it was weighted with lead. Dark crescents of sweat showed under her arms.

Peggy squeezed lime into a bowl of avocados. "You want a beer, Chip?"

"Oh man, yes."

She handed him one from the fridge, then turned and called out across the loft. "Curtis, Chip is here!"

From behind a partition wall, came Curtis' reply: "'kay!"

A moment later Curtis emerged from behind the wall, walking across to the kitchen. "Hey, Chip."

"Hey, man."

Peggy mashed avocados with a fork.

Curtis raised an open beer off the island and took a gulp. "Hot enough for ya?"

"Oh, man! Doesn't this building have a/c?"

"No," Pearl said.

Curtis grinned at Peggy, sitting on a stool, and sneaked a corn chip into the avocados. Peggy slapped his hand away.

"Chip," Peggy said, "Pearl is from Vancouver. She's staying with us while working on a film."

"You're in film?"

Pearl nodded.

"Catering," Peggy said.

"They fly you from Vancouver to Toronto to cater?"

She nodded again, lifting a burning cigarette from an ashtray.

"She's very good," Peggy said, "but she's thinking of moving to L.A. Right, Pearl?"

Pearl blew smoke.

"At the moment she's doing her impersonation of a clam, but don't let it fool you. She's a real shark. She put the bite on a big Hollywood producer just this afternoon. Didn't you, Pearl?"

"Hey, that's funny," Chip said, "I'm thinking of moving to L.A. myself."

Curtis was leaning forward, looking in the paper bag.

"Champagne!" he said, pulling a bottle out of the bag.

Chip smiled. "That director wants to see my treatment."

• • •

THEY LAY COILED together on a pale-pink, kidney-shaped sofa like two beasts descended upon one shell. The time was nearing 3:00 a.m. and all the people were gone. Chip had popped the champagne half an hour ago and it fizzled quietly in glasses on the floor. A red lava lamp, the only light in the room, undulated slowly on the table next to them casting molten shadows across the walls and ceiling. Curtis's huge, round painting – a yellow and gold thing, ten feet high – looked down on them from the opposite wall.

The party had been hot and noisy and crowded. At its peak, some drunk university kid had smashed one of Peggy's vases – a red-and-white one, with cracks all over it – and Curtis had tussled with him and thrown him out, but not before one of the kid's friends had flung a pizza slice at the big painting. The party died after that. The dusty remnants of the vase were swept against the wall and Curtis spent the next hour cleaning the painting. Then he and Peggy went to bed.

It was Pearl who suggested turning off the fans. Outside, a southerly wind had come up blowing cool air off the lake. Thunder rolled across the city and she wanted to hear it. They sat on the sofa, sipping champagne, listening to the rumblings and to their hosts' quietly whispered bedroom sympathies. Then the bedroom went silent and Chip and Pearl soon found themselves entangled in each other's arms.

"I like your earrings," said Chip, lifting one from where it lay against her warm neck.

"Thanks."

It looked like it was molded from a piece of coral. "Are they gold?"

"Yeah."

"Where'd you get them?"

"My mother went to Tahiti last year."

Then, hooking a finger through the hoop in his ear, she said, "I like yours too," and drew his mouth down onto hers.

A siren wailed through the night.

Minutes later, as they separated – flushed, salty, gasping – the great, dark loft fell eerily quiet. All they could hear was their own breathing and the distant white noise of the city. The wind and thunder disappeared, receding as though marshalling its force. A smell like freshly turned soil filled the air. Pearl and Chip lay silent, gazing into one another's eyes. Then, like echoes across the surface of some torpid lagoon, they heard each other ask: "So what's your screenplay about?"

In the bedroom, entangled like fish hooks under the damp sheet on their futon, Curtis and Peggy sank their faces into their pillows, hoping the thunderstorm now exploding overhead would be enough to drown out their laughter.

Evie Christie

THE NIGHTS WE SPEND WITH OTHERS

Are fewer and further between
loneliness and sacrament.
My best friend gave her bottom half
to a skinny bar-back last week,
he crawled between her legs, 2 days drunk,
had to finish herself off, said,
All the same, he was the best I've had
in awhile. We're modestly sober so that our slim lists
fatten when we've had a few – we recount duct tape
and the ties that bound anything that moved.
Open fists, strawberry sundaes, the strange ones
feeding like fawn till you knee them into place
and those who talk about their fathers till dawn.
Time alone makes a woman
do things, think things, would scare you stiff.
I led a married banker to my kitchen counter
and left my mark with tooth and nail.
A young man in Jerusalem
because he had a scar like a ribbon 'round his neck,
because he looked sideways, all eyelash, my way,
and at the time I thought *I could love him.*
Spend a night alone with me, wet my bottle,
light us a smoke, promise not to look me in the eye –
    there's no one
I'd rather be with tonight.

SHARED ACCOMMODATIONS

I'd give my eye teeth for a moment
of quiet. But the eye roves – the eye,
wrist, thigh, whole heart.

The whole heart, blood-slick and heaving
as a cat, nearly alive, packed
with buckshot: sodden and fat and horrifying.

The whole heart, thrashing
gracelessly, on. And just outside
of its understanding, the body – mindful

of nothing, slaughtering, fucking,
drinking, eating. My lonely selves, half-
brothers, sleeping, in separate rooms.

Michael Bryson

THE ADULTERER

HE COULDN'T, UNLESS they were married, he told me. He was seeing a therapist. The therapist asked him about his relationship with his mother. He talked and talked, but the therapist did not find anything unusual. At least, the therapist did not say he had found anything unusual. It was possible the therapist was waiting, baiting him for more information before he made his diagnosis. Last month, the therapist said suddenly, Tell me about your father. He didn't know what to think about the therapist's abrupt change in tactics. Last week, the therapist had asked, Who else is involved here? Who are the players? That's when he decided to come to me, he said. The therapist was the only person with whom he had discussed his situation, he said. Not even the women? I asked him. Not even the women, he said. With them, he had professed love. With them, he had expressed desire. He thought his feelings were authentic, but the therapist had convinced him they were not. The therapist had convinced him his feelings for the women were displaced emotions, but the therapist had not yet discovered the source of the displacement. He was waiting for the therapist to offer a diagnosis, but the therapist only asked more questions. He was thinking about cutting off his relationship with the therapist, but he thought the therapist was close to a breakthrough. If the therapist was close to a breakthrough, it would be stupid for him to stop seeing the therapist. He had asked how close he was to a breakthrough. The therapist had told him these things couldn't be rushed. A breakthrough cannot be willed; it comes of its own accord, and it appears at the end of the path diligently followed. There are many false paths, the therapist said. The false paths help point the way to the true path. It is impossible to tell how many false paths need to be followed before one finds the path leading to the breakthrough. Can I tell you everything? he asked me. When he said this, I saw desperation in his eyes. I told him he could tell me whatever he wished. He told me everything. He said he began sleeping with other men's wives ten years ago after he won $15,000 on a lottery ticket he shared with his co-workers. He was twenty-two then, and very nearly virginal. It was the summer after he dropped out of university, and he didn't know what to do with his life. The lottery money allowed him to pay off his debts and start over. He got a job in a coffee shop and lived in a house with five nursing students. Lusty young women, all of them, he told me. But he did not touch a single one. Instead, he worked the late shift and had sex with his co-worker in the storage room after they locked up. His co-worker was twenty-six and married to a stockbroker. It was more than six months since the stockbroker had made love to her, she said. They were sharing a cigarette at the end of their shift when she said this. Then she kissed him. A month later, the stockbroker was transferred to New York, and that was the last he saw of his co-worker. He thought he loved her. Did you say this to her? I asked. Yes, he said. Many times. But she just said I know you do. She wasn't cold-hearted, he said, but I thought he was just being kind. Quickly, he fell in love again. With another married woman. She smiled at him on the subway. He followed her off the train, up the stairs, and into a nearby bookstore. As she flipped through a cookbook of Mandarin desserts, he stood beside her thumbing through something by Bukowski. She whispered she had silk sheets. She stepped in front of him and felt his erection. An hour later, he was at her apartment flat on his back, his latest lady friend above him, pumping him, bruising him, making him sore. He slept with five different married women that summer, he told me. At the time, he did not see the pattern. He felt simply full of ardor and need. The women came to him; the women left him. At the time, he did not find this troublesome; he did not suffer. For the women, it was not always so easy. One of the women, somewhat melodramatically he thought – and I agreed – called him "the heartbreak angel." The moniker sunk deep into his mind and dug itself like a fishhook into his central vortex, tugging against his brain every time he thought of sex. When he reported this label to his therapist, his therapist asked him: Do you consider yourself a helper? At first, he said no, he did not; but he came to change his mind after his therapist persisted in trumpeting the point. The therapist wore him down, he said, but he wanted me to know that he honestly – although belatedly – agreed with him. His therapist told him: You are a white knight, a savior, a Rambo-type come to save these women from their psychological Vietnams. *Did he actually say that?* I asked. I couldn't believe it. *Their psychological Vietnams?* The therapist often said things like that, he said. He expressed no surprise at the therapist's choice of words. He said he understood the therapist's tone to be part of the therapy. He tries to provoke a reaction from me, he said. He tries to find what I find startling. He said he did not find much that the therapist said startling. He did, once. But he didn't any more. Which was another reason why he was thinking of leaving therapy. Maybe I just haven't met the right woman, he said. Maybe I've just had a run of bad luck. Do you find unmarried women unattractive? I asked. Oh, no, he said. I find them perfectly attractive, but when I find out they're unmarried – I just can't. How strange, I said. Was there more you wanted to tell me? He nodded. So much, he hardly knew where to begin, he said. I could see he was suffering. Every time we met, his constitution seemed diminished. He pulled his cigarettes out of his breast pocket and lit one. The first time we had met like this, he had been close to tears. I had walked him home, and left him with a hug. Since then his skin had become paler, his shoulders more slouched. I had given him the number of my cell phone, and he had called me twelve times in the following two days. Six times my husband answered, only to be met with a dial tone. You must be careful in the future, I told him the next time we met. Wait for me to call you. He had felt compelled to talk to me, he said. He had felt himself withering, fragmenting, drying up like paint flaking off a wall. He had felt himself falling, in need of a soft landing. All he could think of was calling me, he said. I said I understood (I had wanted to call him, too), but I also reminded him of the need to be more careful. I felt closer to him than to anyone in a long time. My husband knew nothing, and could never know anything, I told him. He said he understood. He had the softest hands. You must give up your therapist, I told him. You must speak of this only to me. He said he agreed. I was the only one he felt saw the real him. I was the only one who asked him to be transparent, and I was the only one he had ever felt truly naked before. You can have no others before me, I told him. He was on his knees in front of me when I said this. He was sobbing lightly, but he nodded. Yes, he said. Yes, yes. Oh, yes.

Rob Winger

RE-COVERING CHAMPLAIN TRAILS

all poems must include the following:

your sensitive talent for discovering spring:
the signature tulips, insightfully soggy clouds,
inflatable metaphors over lookouts, overlooking the Canadian
Club bottles littering the constructed
escarpment you figure
as virgin,
leaving interpretive plaques and other tourists
out
and your eventual collapse from that exclusive
connection to the sublime.

how you trace the national Anglo-Canadian
Shield with grandiose comments on time on history on invented
        fossils,
on tiny, historic Frenchmen who ate sea turtles,
one-dimensional wildlife bursting into your special conditions of
postmodernity, bearclaw cherry tree, beaver dam,
sugarbush woodpeckers, red hawks looming in the turgid updraft
figured as symbol, as death (plop!), as your plucking of the first red
trilliums from the syrupy undergrowth with a triumphant squeeze
of pliers.

the apex, where you edit out a flawless man-
made bench, exclude a tattered copy of *The Idiot*,
phrases faded, ugly pages drenched,
spine reeking fungus,
tossed into sage scrub;

the apex, where you look deeply into distant
Holsteins scattered across hot checkerboard vistas and omit
their patties from your songs of pure
forest, of solitary genius, of the man
of feeling, of heroic, historic methods for
clearing ground.

a penultimate plastic umbrella for your
brimful goblet of saccharine
scenery, and, finally, one, last, punch
line on lacklustre clouds, on everyday wind,
on the unwanted flowers you squash beneath
those sensitive two-hundred-dollar
soles of yours.

RE-CONSTITUTING THE FAMILY

Everything happens again and it's never the same.
  – Ethel Wilson as Nell Severence

1.
here's the one when you discover genetics
when, ankle-deep in faded mothball
archival records you find a link to your second
arrivals

parents are compared to national
stereotypes with scotch with
golf with saris with monsoons or cricket
or Afrikaans with the geographical lexicons
you've just learned

a generational photograph tells you
something here is essential, so
you trace present biology, what's left
over from holds and burying grounds and
maps.

2.
the one where you lament lost grandparents, pets, famous uncles,
pointless political crusades,
where you relate the broken
cheekbones of fundamentalist men at bars, the secret
rapes of grandmothers that mean your blood is
mixed

the one where certain lines are interrupted by bullets.

3.
the one where the ship's hold is fecal mess
and gangrene and colourful national poverties,
tar and pitch and roll

the one where the land first rises at Ellis Island / Grosse Île
where you read Susanna's first view of bush,
syllables dripping from custom officers with rifles

the one where someone clears the trees.

4.
the one with the graveyard, with syllables eaten
by orange moss, with cement broken into triangles,
with caskets

the one where you return to an empty field and enforce
visions of the paternal line, of gaslight and horses,
of winters without furnaces

the one with histories.

5.
the one, for me, on the Walpole Township crop farm
where the fields are unforgiving and clichéd and true and
the great great grandfather figure is a bearded drunk who means
what he preaches before being excommunicated from
his congregation   before his   consummation

the one where he's tied to his horse at the Hagersville Hotel and
carried ten concessions home beneath the
Southwestern Ontario constellations

the one where his wife's name gets erased.

6.
the one where you say
go fuck yourself with your Atom bomb.

7.
the one that's feminist, racist, sexist, sugarist
the one that's passé, incorrect, insensitive, ahistorical
the one where what's real and what's right
are at odds, are odd, come in against the odds of
what will really carry weight,
what will assemble into a weighty school of thought,
your desire for something elsewhere and true.

the one where simple muscles harness
the pure earth.

Matthew J Trafford

THORACIC EXAM

THE PATIENT'S NAME is Kennedy Slippington.

She sits before me on the table wearing a standard gown like any other patient. Ms. Slippington, brunette, has her hair pulled up away from her neck and shoulders. She looks to me like the type of woman who, upon entering middle age, is careful to have all the most thorough medical examinations as a preventative measure against disease, a self-care practice that as a nurse I admire and promote. I check her file briefly and see that she has not presented with any unusual pain or respiratory distress and is not taking medication – facts I check with her verbally to make certain.

Unsurprisingly, she is a non-smoker and exercises regularly. It has been a year since her last in-depth thoracic exam. I ask her to lower her gown to the waist, and I begin.

There are many things most people don't know about the lungs. That the apex of each lung, for example, extends slightly above the clavicle. That the base of each lung sits far higher than is generally thought – at the tenth rib, about halfway down the back. Many nurses who have not kept up with their training end up auscultating much lower than they should, in effect listening to the diaphragm or viscera. Many nurses also neglect the lateral portion of the examination, which yields important access to the right middle lobe. I have recently upgraded my credentials in night school.

I decide to perform the tests involving the stethoscope first, because I know it is at room temperature and I fear my fingers may still be cold from going outside at lunch. I do not wish to make her uncomfortable. I explain what I am about to do. I ask her to repeat either '99' or 'blue moon,' the two standard phrases set by medical practitioners to create measurable resonance.

"Blue moon," she says, as I move the stethoscope along its prescribed path, left side, right side, right side, left, checking for the proper bronchophony. "Blue moon. Blue moon." And then she sobs so violently it hurts my ears and the lurch of her diaphragm is visible to the naked eye.

"I'm sorry," she articulates, "I'm so sorry." She brings her hands to her face quickly, then seems to change her mind and starts wiping her eyes and inspiring her mucous loudly. "My husband – he died recently. He – he used to jump out of planes. You know, skydive, as a hobby. I never liked him to do it, but he was stubborn. Oh, was he ever." She bangs her hands on the table then brings them to her face again, then lowers them to her lap and looks up at me. "His parachute failed to open during his last jump. He was in Vermont. All I got was a phone call: *Are you Mrs. Theodore Michael Pratt?* They had to ship the body – and – and now that's it, there's just nothing. No investigation, no liability, no reason. He's gone, and it's something I'm supposed to just accept. That this type of accident happens all the time." By this point her lachrymal ducts are secreting tears, and I can hear by her voice that her sinuses have started to fill. "I'm sorry," she says again, "I'm sorry."

In front of her, my stomach has filled with liquid ether and my knees are trembling so hard I have grabbed the table for support.

This isn't sympathy.

• • •

I AM NINETEEN again in Prague, city of the thousand spires, unspoiled by war and flaunting a gorgeous tapestry of paradox: old and new, Byzantine and Renaissance, atheist and Hussite and Catholic and Jewish, communist and nascent capitalist, subterranean and alpine. At this age I still believe art matters, am still content to spend my time wrangling with colour and line and form, or clumsily cobbling words together to make poems, sitting in countless underground bars illuminated solely by the glow of Pilsner beer and men's smiles, wearing black and discussing Truth or Politics while smoking vanilla-scented tobacco from South American countries, crossing and uncrossing my legs and trying always to appear witty, fey, or beautiful.

I couldn't get enough of life back then: strawberries exploded in my mouth with the sweet prick of love and possibility, I drank wine by the bottle and dipped dense dumplings in goulash twice a day, took an assortment of men to my bed with abandon and true revelling in the joy of my own body, until I met Theo. Theo, who everyone had mentioned as either a hero or an asshole, who had been there since the Curtain fell, who now ran the prominent English newspaper and pursued serious journalism, and who I finally met at a reading in December when the cobblestones were covered with snow that glistened in the headlights of trams trundling through the night. Theo, who repeatedly ran fingers through his dark, tousled hair when nervous, whose dimple was shy and unpredictable, who always looked mischievous, Theo who warned me about his native Missouri and any state with a boot-heel or a panhandle, and who debated with me for hours about the pronunciation of 'wabe' in the Jabberwocky poem. Theo, who once told me about his unbridled passion for collage, manically cutting from magazines and newspapers and tourist brochures and pasting together mosaics of high-gloss irony, whose early poems in the now-defunct literary magazines were superlative and had the mark of the farm boy he once was in them – cows, rattlesnakes, barns – who would come out to cavernous music clubs only to sit and resist the beat, who only danced once, at his best friend's birthday party, joining us and swaying with his hands on his pelvis, holding them up and angled inwards like a háček, almost crude, who excited me and paralyzed me and who never ever made the first move.

Who once shared with me three small bottles of Becherovka, that golden Czech liqueur that tastes of Christmas, distilled from pine needles and smelling of cinnamon, as he slowly unbuttoned his shirt and put on ridiculous straw hats we'd bought in the flea markets near the Florenc bus station, and we took our shoes off and rubbed each other's feet, and I dared to ask about his tattoo: a crescent moon, tattooed in corn-flower blue above his left nipple. Like him it was gorgeous but seemed unfinished somehow – a little too pale, a slight waver in the lines – and he had the air of a man disclosing a deep secret, or else I willfully mistook regret as confessional intimacy, while he told me: "I was really drunk one night in college – they're not supposed to give you tattoos when you're drunk. Across the street there was some insurance company, and this was their logo. I just looked out the window and told the guy to put it on my chest." I wanted to ask if he was wearing a shirt when he walked into the parlour, because to me it seemed like the most important detail, the detail that would lead to tracing the tattoo with the tip of my tongue, grazing his nipple with my teeth, kissing the hollow of his breastbone and let-ting gravity and drunkenness and sheer desire pull my mouth lower and lower, but I collapsed into giggles or hiccoughs or vomiting or else I simply passed out before I could.

Theo, who one winter night, drunk and warm with good food and a glow of superiority, walked me home from a poetry reading at Shakespeare and Sons Bookstore Café, down Krymská and through the narrow streets, with snowflakes the size of saucers falling on his navy pea coat, catching in his hair, on his eyelashes, and in front of my doorway leaned in and kissed me, his thin moist lips pressing against my fuller ones for three hard seconds, until he pulled away with a pleased look on his face, and instead of following me inside said "Have a good night, kid" and got into a taxi and left.

Who was the reason I left Prague defeated, because he never mentioned that kiss again or paid enough attention to me to satisfy, because I could never ask him why he turned away or tell him how desperately I wanted him, because I hated myself for that and hated him for not seeing it and loving me or wanting me or at the very, very least, offering me an explanation of why not.

• • •

"Ms. Slippington," I say, "please pull yourself together." I coil the stethoscope and lay it on the counter. I take a deep breath, and turn back to her.

I continue the exam by rote, my fingers moving like mechanized rods. I palpate the skin, checking for lumps, bumps, lesions, discoloration, cyanosis. What I long to see now are the puckered scars of cigarette burns, raised welts, bruising. Some sign her life has included trauma, chronic pain. I want to see proof that Theo abused her, that having him was poisonous to her. Or else I want to find evidence of why she was more worthy of him than me. Yet everything about her remains standard. Her costal angle is exactly ninety degrees.

I begin to auscultate her anterior thorax. The first two fingers of my left hand against her chest, then a quick rap on the first knuckles with the index finger of my right, a little harder than I should. First position. Second. I locate the angle of Louis.

I ask her to raise and separate her breasts, and auscultate between them on either side of the sternum. My fingers leave round white impressions that fade instantly when I move my fingers away. Her skin is dry and I wonder how often he licked her sweat from this place, or from her suprasternal notch. I wonder if she ever held her breasts like this while he fucked her from behind. I put my hand on her wrist to show she can let go.

I move to her posterior thorax. I place my hand gently on her head and angle it forward. At the nape of her neck the bone rises beneath the skin, C7, the *vertebra prominens*. I can see how he would have bent his head and kissed her here. I want to place my lips around this bone, feel its contours between my teeth, and puncture the flawless skin. If I were to slice her in this place she would be wheelchair-bound for life. There are scalpels less than three feet away.

Instead I auscultate her back, desperate to find something unusual, anything. I imagine a raised mole with suspicious edges, an adipose cyst, a patch of eczema. I imagine his name tattooed above her left kidney, or a crescent blue moon to match his under her shoulder blade. She is maddeningly blank. Worse, I can find no sign of him. I want to touch him again in some small way, want her body to bring his back to me.

At my behest she places her hands on her head, so I can examine her laterally. I think immediately of handcuffs and girdles. Theo hog-tied beneath a whip-wielding Ms. Slippington. His tongue gliding across her black patent-leather boot. I picture him watching her from bed as she ties her hair up each morning, takes it down each night before coming to join him.

I rush a little across the room and snatch up the stethoscope again, not because it's required but because I must eavesdrop inside of her. I am no longer assessing normal breath sounds, bronchial or vesicular, or checking for wheezing or crackles in the peripheral lobes. I'm just listening to this woman breathe in and out, inflation and deflation of pink alveoli, closing my eyes and hearing the air rush in and out of her body, knowing that Theo has breathed in unison with this woman, shared breath with her and been inside her.

Finally, I perform a diaphragmatic excursion, a difficult test most nurses omit through ignorance or lack of skill. I am being very, very thorough. This is Theo's wife. She has gained and lost what I never even came close to. Everything about her is normal.

"I'm finished," I say, "You can put your robe back on." She complies as I pick up her chart again and uncap my pen. I press hard when I sign my name and go over and over my signature until I am afraid the paper will tear. I arrange my face into a professional expression of sympathy and concern. "I hate to be the bearer of bad news, but there is a problem with your right lung. I'm hearing adventitious and abnormal breathing sounds with decreased airflow, and the responses there are dull instead of resonant. I can't tell you anything for certain, of course, but these symptoms are usually indicative of a growth in the lungs, in your case a rather substantive mass of tissue. I'll notify your physician immediately, and he'll follow up with you to arrange for further testing, an x-ray and a biopsy and whatever else may be deemed necessary."

Kennedy Slippington looks at me with dilated pupils, her face paler now than when we started. Her eyebrows have knit together, as though she is concentrating very intently on a mental task, recognizing a forgotten scent, translating awkward phrases from a foreign language. Her jaw is slack so that her mouth hangs open, revealing her perfect teeth. "Oh my God," she whispers. "Oh my." And then, extremely softly, "Thank you for telling me."

I hold her gaze for three seconds, then turn from her; my heart rate accelerates and my chest constricts. This is the first time I have turned my back on a patient in distress, knowingly hurt someone. There will probably be consequences.

But then again, hospitals are large and crowded places. This type of accident happens all the time.

David Livingstone Clink

THE SIX-LEGGED DOG RETRIEVES A STICK

If you didn't see the six-legged dog it doesn't matter. He mostly lay in the corner, mad with magic anger. When I watched him I stopped living. It was then, at that moment, or another, the keeper threw a stick and the dog went after it, on four legs, the other two flapping behind, useless, which made one girl shriek with laughter. After that, I quit shaving; razors seemed too sharp to me, and daydreaming felt like a nod to a future all used up.

How different everything might have been if that dog had only four legs! My attention would have been on the drunk woman, or the man who could put his entire fist in his mouth, who was also drunk: he kept kissing her neck, following her around the Fair. Or I might have noticed the baton-twirling snakes, *The All Muskrat Marching Band*, or the weather, which was a mix of sun and clowns. Or I might have noticed you. But that was not the case. My attention was squarely on the six-legged dog. It retrieved the stick, and looked back at us, and that was the whole show.

You never saw the dog. You were looking at me while I was remembering how you were most yourself when swimming: slicing the water with each stroke; how you tried to keep pace with me – you were neither fantastic nor miserable when doing laps, the funny way you breathed, your mouth cocked as though yawning. When I look back I remember how I thought at the time you were moving too slowly to save me, but I realize now you were moving as fast as you could.

THE TIME OF THE YOUNG SOLDIERS

Time
A time apart: letters of love and war
A time for anger: the myth of neutrality
 for courage: the Royal Air Force in the European War,
  1939–1945
A time for drunken horses

A time for listening and caring: spirituality and the care of the
 chronically ill and dying
A time for peace
A time of fear, a novel
 The time of freedom
  of her life: a novel

 The time of my life: entertaining the troops, her wartime
 journals
The time of the young soldiers
  of their dying
Time on our side: growing in wisdom, not growing old
Time to bite the bullet

A time to embrace
  to hear, a time to help: listening to people with cancer
A time to kill
  to love
  to mourn
Time to remember
Time to say goodbye.

Alayna Munce

ROMANCE

It was by my mother's decree: a valentine for every last one, the whole class list, even Anthony who smelled like pee. Of course, there was still a certain valentine I took stealthy extra time with, pouring all my nine-year-old love into my penmanship, not spilling a drop. And though every year since there's been one valentine I've troubled over beyond all the rest,

this year I'm wondering what would happen if I abided by more than the letter of the law. If I submitted myself to a new decree, its loopholes slimmer. If I poured my hoard into the whole damn list:

painstaking penmanship for everyone. For my friend Alex, for instance, who says, *That's okay, if you get to be our age and you're not at least a little bit wounded and scarred,*

you're not paying attention. And for Johanne, who says when she was broken-hearted it helped her to think that there was suffering out there that had to be suffered, like there was garbage that had to be removed, dishes that had to be done. That she was just doing her part. The thought made pain a task, matter of fact. All she had to do was think the thought and her life widened swiftly like a pupil expanding when the lights are turned, mercifully,

off. And for my grandfather. For how we go out for Chinese and he buys lottery tickets with the fortune cookie numbers. How he informs me over lurid chicken balls that Tim Horton's has raised the price of a coffee by five cents. How he shakes his head and leans in. *I'll tell you what that is,* he whispers. *Pure greed.* A valentine for the fact

that he can be scandalized. That he can be scandalized means there's some alternative. And one for the bartender we call the Colonel. How he says, *There's rubber-stamp time,*

and then there's flying time. I, of course, want it all to be flying time – is that greedy or just wet behind the ears?

A valentine for that phrase, wet-behind-the-ears. Whenever I hear it I think of Hildegaard von Bingen, the 12th century saint who signed her letters off,

Stay moist. And one for the fact that almost anyone will feel delight at finding strangely shaped root vegetables in the garden. And even more so in the bins of grocery stores. Carrots intertwined. Deviant potatoes shaped like hearts.

And one for the abandoned innards of a turntable I saw on the sidewalk yesterday. How it seemed to me the thing should be able to tell the time,

like a sundial. And for how I looked up from the turntable and noticed for the first time that the dirty little laneway – the one that runs between the Church of the Epiphany and the No *Loitering* signs at the public library – that lane is called

Milky Way. How it leads to the abandoned Star Aluminium Factory. And one for how yesterday Johanne went to the dollar store, bought a heart-shaped cake pan (called, "The All-Occasion Heart"), and made me a cake to cheer me up. How over tea and cake she spoke about her son's startling talent for writing stories in the horror genre, how he's got a motherlode of darkness to be transformed. How last year, when his novella was published, he reminded her of something she'd said during one of his dark times: *Everybody's got more than their share of something.*

And for how this makes me look differently at the obese lady labouring heroically down the street under all that weight.

And my friend Ruth who, with six loved ones dying in a span of six months, was pummelled by grief into one of the supplest people I know.

And Michael who has visions of the ultimate reconciliation so pure and intense he sometimes believes he's the saviour and has to be hospitalized. How the last time Michael went psychotic my ex-husband (who was still my husband at the time) came with me to visit, and Michael had on his windowsill an elaborate collage of colours and words and naked limbs torn from Cosmopolitan magazine, a collage he warned us not to touch, not to even go near enough to breathe on. How he looked around to make sure no one was listening then whispered, *It may contain some very important secrets.* How he was lost for a moment then in a long besotted stare at the arrangement of loose scraps on his windowsill. How when he came out of it he began, regal in his backless hospital gown, to arrange us, my then-husband and I, so that we were sitting side by side on his hospital bed, looking through his narrow window at the night sky. And he arranged our arms so that we were holding hands, arranged us like dolls. And he made us keep looking out the window at the sky and backed away until he was in the corner of the room. And when I glanced over at him he pointed harshly back at the window. And when we'd sat there like that long enough to get a little past the strangeness and discomfort and begin to actually look at the stars,

Michael said from his corner,

Now you two go home and make love to each other like it's the last night on earth.

And for how something greedy in me can't help wishing we all had Michael there to arrange us every night.

Thirteen years ago yesterday I met my now-ex-husband. We used to joke at parties about how unimaginative it was of us to have met on Valentine's Day, but the truth is

we both secretly loved it. Anyway, one idea of romance is finished, like a task, and is quickly replaced by another. We move on. Or rather, we're moved on. No loitering. Often we move on limping, as if in a three-legged race: one side of us bound, holding on tight, rubber stamping toward the finish line; the other side wild and flapping, as if trying to get free. Though occasionally there is flying time. Right now

I'm working on a valentine for how, on the way to yesterday's cake, I actually had to stop and stare at the Milky Way sign. How I stood there in the cold on the sidewalk for a second, greedy for more than my share of something I can't quite name. Stood still, as if to say,

> *Don't breathe on it; it may contain some very important secrets.*

Leigh Kotsilidis

SELF-DESTRUCTION MANUAL: BRIDGE JUMPER

Empty your pockets, there's a river
rushing toward you from below. Throw
paper items first. Let birds gather
torn notes, make a nest out of knowing
you couldn't make it. Next, toss your watch.
Time it well, a fisherman struck down
could make your last moments hell. Now,
rid yourself of coins, cigarettes, gum.
Then, move on to weighty items – this could
buy you time to lose the shoes. Though be sure
to save the heaviest possession for
the final fling – in case you change your mind.
This will burst the water's tension open
so your whole body may slip in unharmed.

THE WAY THE COOKIE CRUMBLED

Heart-slumped, bushwhacked
taxed, adrift, sunk
defunct, done for, null
and void, overboard
cut loose without a paddle
kicked out, smashed in
sucker-punched, ditched
bottom-hitched, broke
missed the boat, smoked
drawn and quartered, deboned
head held in the gutter
picked clean, creamed, tossed
like a salad left to the wolves
throat slit, cajoled with, stabbed
in the ransacked back, cut off
at the knees up to the eyeballs
butchered, wing clipped
stripped and bullwhipped, crushed
like a grape strung out
to dry, fed to the lions, fired
to a crisp, knuckle-
sandwiched, holding on
with nothing left
to bruise.

Heather J Wood

50 WAYS, MY ASS!

PAUL SIMON LIED to me back in '76. Twenty-four hours before my Valentine birthday, my not quite nine-year-old self was alarm-clocked into consciousness by "Slip out the back, Jack. Make a new plan, Stan…"

I didn't actually have to worry about leaving lovers in grade three, but I figured that Paul was offering me some important advice for when I was old, like nineteen. After all, even Sony and Cher had split up.

That night Dorothy Hamill and her bouncing haircut twirled their way to the Olympic gold medal. My brother was with me in the TV room, pretending that he wasn't watching Dorothy's ass in her perky pink skirt.

"Um, Greg…."

"Yeah, twerp?"

"I know what you can get me for my birthday."

"A Bionic Woman T-shirt?"

"Sit on it," I said, full-on Fonzie style. "I want a record. A real one, not like the K-tel you got me at Christmas. I heard it on the radio this morning – *50 Ways to Leave Your Lover*."

"Whatever you say, kiddo," said Greg, still leering at Dorothy's legs. "Although *Donny & Marie's Greatest Hits* would probably be more your speed."

My brother somehow avoided being his usual jerk self and bought me Paul Simon's number one hit. It came on a whole album, but I never listened to the other songs. I just kept picking up the turntable needle and re-playing *50 Ways* over and over again. After my 232nd listen, I realized there was a problem. Paul hadn't actually listed anything close to fifty ways. In fact he'd only mentioned about five options. But I still thought

Paul was telling the truth back then. I hoped he was saving the other forty-five for a sequel.

• • •

Twenty years and almost six months later, I was getting ready for our 100-metre dash bash. "Donovan Bailey's gonna kick American ass in Atlanta tonight," Liam had announced over coffee that morning. "We've gotta have an Olympic-sized party."

Liam and I first hooked up at Lollapalooza '93 – that was the year most of the bands sucked. An Eddie Vedder look-alike, he noticed my sea green Docs in the concession line. "Nice boots," he said. "They match your eyes. I'm Liam – wanna fuck?" It was love at first blurry sight.

Our third anniversary was two weeks ago. I gave Liam Nirvana's *Unplugged*. He was running out to get me a gift when his friends invited themselves over for an impromptu party. One of them smashed my Chuck and Di mug, figuring it was worthless now that they were getting divorced.

The apartment was still a wreck from that party. Liam won the coin toss, so he was doing the munchies and beer shopping. I was stuck dealing with the smell of stale Heineken wafting from the carpet and the half-empty pizza boxes rotting in the kitchen. Liam was unemployed again and could have tidied up earlier, but as with job-hunting and gift-giving, he never managed to get around to it.

To pump myself up for hours of vacuuming, fumigating and ashtray-emptying, I turned on the radio, poured some Coke into my Krazy Glued Chuck and Di mug and flipped open the pack of Player's on the coffee table. But the pack was empty – the shit had taken my last smoke.

I cranked the radio volume up to ten. Familiar lyrics boomed through the living room "Hop on the bus, Gus. You don't need to discuss much..."

"Bullshit, Paul. There aren't fifty ways to leave your lover," I yelled at the speakers. "Just one."

I ripped my empty cigarette pack apart and flattened it on the table. With a pink highlighter pen, I wrote Dear Liam, goodbye and fuck you. Love, Sue.

Then I walked out the door and set myself free.

I KILLED YOUR CACTUS

SALLY SCANNED THE apartment before making the call. Everything seemed to be in order. Everything except for the contents of a small green pot on the windowsill.

"I killed your cactus," she told Evan over the phone.

"What?"

"That little plant," Sally said sheepishly. "The sort of phallic-looking one. I assume it was a cactus. It's wilted and lost its colour."

"My red top. How could you manage that?"

"I watered it too much... or something."

"Is Mr. Feldman OK? Or did you manage to kill him, too?"

Sally glanced over at the sleeping mass of grey fur on the sofa. It appeared to be breathing. "The cat's fine," she said. "He still doesn't like me but he's fine. He wants you back, though."

There was a loud chuckle at the other end of the line. "I hope you want me back too."

"Of course," Sally said.

After the phone conversation was over, it occurred to Sally that she might have lied. She wanted Evan to come back because she'd had enough of cat and plant responsibilities. But did she really want him to come back to her?

She picked up a blue T-shirt, the one that Evan had left hanging over the back of his ancient reclining chair. The shirt smelled of him. His salty sweat, his musky aftershave, his bacon and coffee breakfasts. It was Evan's morning shirt – the one he put on after jumping out of bed. He'd change it later after cooking and eating. Evan had a nighttime shirt too. He'd put in on when he wanted to sleep. Just sleep.

Sally never let him make breakfasts in her own kitchen. She hated the heavy smell and the way grease would infect the air. Bacon reminded her of when she and her sister got food poisoning. It was three months after their mother had deserted them, and their father had decided it was time to tackle the domestic duties.

"I've made us a cooked breakfast, girls." Dad had been wearing a faded flower-patterned apron and was forcing a large smile.

Sheila pushed her food away. "The eggs look weird," she said. "You broke the yolks."

"Makes them easier to digest," said Dad. "They don't have to get broken up inside you."

"But the bacon smells funny," Sally said, sniffing her plate.

Their father's large smile dissolved into a frown, so the girls stopped their complaints and nibbled on their meal in silence. A few hours later, they each took turns throwing up in the downstairs bathroom. Sally's insides were still throbbing when her father brought a mug of chicken noodle soup to her room. "It's been hard going for all of us," he told her. "But things will get better if you give it a chance."

• • •

THE MORNING AFTER Sally first spent the night at his place, Evan had prepared bacon, beans and scrambled eggs. Sally wandered into the kitchen yawning, just as Evan finished pouring the bacon drippings into an old orange juice can. The odour of grease permeated the room.

"Hope you're hungry," he said, pointing at the mounds of food on the table.

Sally gave him a quick kiss on the forehead. "Um, I usually just have coffee and something light. I don't really do cooked breakfasts."

"It's a good thing I'm extra hungry," Evan said, patting his stomach.

He rummaged through his cupboards, looking for breakfast alternatives. Sally was offered a box of sickly sweet cereal, one that would have been forbidden by her mother. Following the food poisoning incident, she and Sheila had been allowed to eat any breakfast they wanted. But the novelty soon wore off and a familiar guilt took over. "We only want to eat the cereals that Mum said we're OK," they announced during their third month of Cap'n Crunch.

Evan eventually solved their breakfast dilemma. "Hot croissants for you. Bacon and eggs for me," he announced when he first discovered the delights of a nearby bakery. "Now both of us can be happy in the mornings."

• • •

SALLY WAS FIVE minutes late meeting her sister for their weekly cafe date. Sheila had already ordered for both of them when Sally arrived.

"Sorry, I got held up at Evan's place."

"At least you have an excuse this time," said Sheila, checking her watch. "So what happens when he gets back? Are the two of you ever going to live together?"

Sally picked up a spoon and stirred her coffee with unnecessary precision. "Don't know yet."

"You've got to settle down sometime."

"Evan wants to. But what if things don't work out?"

"Not everyone is like our parents," said Sheila. "Which reminds me, I've been meaning to tell you something. Bob and I are going to ask Dad to move in with us."

"You've got to be kidding."

"His latest contract is coming to an end and he's stopped seeing his girlfriend. He could help me look after the kids. It would do him good."

"Right. I'm going to get a refill." Sally thought her father had done more than his share of childrearing, but she wasn't about to argue with Sheila. Her little sister had grown up to be the responsible one. Sheila knew about plants and pets and long-term relationships.

Milk and sugar usually fortified Sally's coffee, yet she left her second cup black. Sheila droned on about her new household plans, but Sally barely took in any of her sister's words. She was too surprised by the intense pleasure she was experiencing from her dark drink. On her birthday, Evan had cheered her up with a homemade chocolate cake. Sally had dreaded reaching thirty-six, the age her mother was when she disappeared, but it was as if Evan's warm presence had melted Sally's fears away. He'd encouraged her to enjoy the cake with black coffee. "It enhances the flavour and makes everything clearer," he said.

It was a warm afternoon so Sally turned down her sister's offer of a drive home. "I'm going to walk," she said, clutching a black coffee to go. "I need to move." She was soon back in Evan's neighborhood, and found herself heading towards his apartment.

The cat was waiting behind the door when Sally opened it. In previous visits he had greeted her by digging his claws into her calf. This time he simply rubbed his head against her shin.

"You're not starting to like me, are you, Mr. Feldman? I must be part of the family now."

Mr. Feldman scurried back to his usual spot on the sofa. Sally considered following him when her attention was diverted to the green pot on the windowsill. The cactus was looking a little redder.

Sally had intended to throw the plant away, but instead she decided to help it grow.

Matthew Tierney

PARELASIPHOBIA
(*fear of parades*)

As if real life
weren't Byzantine enough.
Under a xenon-charged sky, floats

float by. A high school band sweats out
Sgt. Pepper epaulettes
and worsted slacks, bleating

a half-tempo "When the Saints
Go Marching In," while the majorettes
in red-spangled spandex

wait in formation, puffy arms poised,
for batons to fall like fallen
angels –

– a go-kart zips past,
Methuselah in a fez, shepherding
fellow Lions Club members

in their tramp to the end.
A peril of fools. Nonsense
is Munchkinland: only

the unfocused, peripheral eye
catches the curls of green
smoke, the long road lined

with scarecrows.

OPTIC NERVE

Evenings, I crisscross King Street
and avoid the panhandlers, spare a glance
to see whether I'm being

tailed. My route, plotted on the xy axis,
tracks supply and demand
to its conclusion. Home

and tired, throwing out flyers, charitable appeals,
free gym memberships. Impulse is
formulaic. Over time

I will take my place in line
alongside the velvet rope. This is who I am:
perforated packaging, disposable contacts,

a healthy platelet count. Sum
equal to the parts. Off the subway at 6:07 p.m.,
every heartbeat disperses

2.4 ounces of blood, retina
converting wavelengths of the visible
into electrical pulses, I weave

my way towards the exit. A stray hand
sifts coins in my pocket,
capillaries flood with the oxygen necessary

for survival. Topside, empty coffee cups
in fists, like white-lipped howls.
The lightless figures behind them.

Kathryn Kuitenbrouwer

THE DEVIL TAKE ME

HE ARRIVED MID-AUGUST with a heavy black bicycle at the
end of the laneway; I was watching him from the kitchen
window. It was as if he arrived, just like that, out of thin air,
two hundred kilometers from the international airport, ten
kilometers from the nearest town, three from the nearest
hydro line. We were expecting him, naturally, a visitor from
Flanders. He was welcome. All that is true, but how he got
there I never asked. His name was André. He had jet-black
hair, an immaculate complexion, and an out of kilter way of
moving, as if there might be something odd with his legs. He
smiled, though I do not believe he could see me, and lugged
his camouflage rucksack up the sandy lane to the stone house,
then turned and went back for the bicycle.

I had left the front door open, and he simply walked in.
"Hi," he said, and sat across from me in a chair Joshu and I
had salvaged from the local dump. It was a pine chair, made
in a vernacular style, with a broken rung and chipped blue
paint; we intended to repair it, just as we intended to repair
any number of other items. He was wearing a thin trench coat,
black, and wore beneath it – I saw when he pulled it off and
let it fall – a white T-shirt and a pair of faded, cut-off denim
shorts. He was clutching something in his fist. He said, "It is
nice of you to let me stay here."

Joshu was at work and the baby was sleeping. André
opened his hand and let fall a fragrant bundle of flowers. They
smelled sweetly acrid. Chamomile, I thought. "Shall I make
tea?" he said.

"Yes."

"I learned how to make this tea with the monks in Spain. I was a year there. We built a stone wall and they would take their tea in this special way. I will make it for you." He went into our rudimentary kitchen and searched around for a kettle. We did not have one and I thought to tell him, but then didn't. It was amusing to watch him struggle with the space, to watch him make-do. It went like this: he filled a pot with water and frigged with the gas knob until he realized the pilot was out, he rummaged in a drawer and then looked all about the counter for a match, or a lighter. "Lucifers?" he said, and I only stared at him and then slowly shook my head, looked confused. I knew that 'lucifers' was the Flemish word for 'matches,' and I admit now to enjoying this bit of intentional confusion. I think I even smiled.

He went over to his rucksack near the door and opened a side pocket, fished around until he located a silver Zippo. He passed by the table and carefully pushed the blossoms into his open palm; I had never seen someone boil flowers to make tea, and thought it primitive. But when it was made I had to admit it was delicious, he'd added milk and honey.

"What is your plan?" I asked.

"I will stay with you and then I will leave on a journey. I have canvas and a needle and thread with which to make a tent. With my bicycle, I will journey out from here."

"A pilgrimage," I suggested.

"I do not know this word."

I tried to explain it but he only looked queerly at me, asked whether I liked the tea. I told him I did, that it was soothing, that I had never tasted anything like that before. The baby woke up then, fiercely. I hadn't wanted a baby; neither of us had, really, but what could we do but accept our own entwining for what it wrought. We had named the girl Magda, after a relative and we pronounced it with the soft Flemish 'g'. She liked to scream, Magda did, and I had read how it was good for the lungs of young babies to do this, so I endured these bracketed outbursts, though they cut to the very soul. "She is very beautiful," André said. The truth was she had both our worst features. I believe André only wished me to pick the child up, to coddle her, to make the noise stop, but I did not. I told him instead how Joshu would be home within the hour, and asked him if he wouldn't mind fetching water from the well; our pump had collapsed, or maybe it was that our generator had broken. Something was always broken. André was happy to help, he said so. I gave him a large plastic bucket and watched him through the window as he struggled with the hand pump at the well, and then as he tried to maintain balance and not spill the water out of the full pail. He had a buoyancy that I was not used to.

I made a soup for dinner and while it simmered I nursed Magda. It was always incredible to watch her suckle; she looked as if she had privately invented it. Joshu called her smarmy, called her Magda the Smarmy. And like I had said, within the hour he was home, kissing me on the cheek, staring down at the baby at my tit, and patting my head. André was out walking the Crown land across the street. He had asked leave to wander off, which naturally tickled me, that he'd asked permission. "You may go," I had said, and gestured regally. He only thanked me, turned and left.

I spied on him, more or less, as he loped over the open field toward the pine forest. He had a fine rear, is what went through my mind, and then I saw Joshu's motorbike and waved as if I had been watching out for him all along. I was sitting in the upholstered wingback that we'd inherited from Joshu's uncle. It stunk of tobacco smoke.

"What's he look like?" he asked.

"He looks like a little devil."

But when André returned Joshu seemed to like him. And why not? The boy had an armful of chanterelles, and some other mushrooms that I did not recognize. "To eat," he said, and began rubbing the soil from them. He took a skillet out of the dish rack and lit the element again with his lighter.

"What about these ones?" I asked. "These suspect fungi?"

"To eat," he said. "I will eat first and then you will eat."

In bed, later, Joshu waggled his hand between my legs and whispered, "Suspect fungi. You and your suspect fungi." We made love spoon style with the baby wedged in at my belly. We were as quiet as we could be under any circumstances but still half way through or so, we heard André shuffling about and then the front door opening and closing.

"I've just finished with a girlfriend," he told me the next day. Joshu was already gone to work and we were at breakfast. "It was a very bad relationship in the end and so I went to the monks at the monastery to see if it might work for me to be a priest. Only I want to marry one day so now I am looking at the orthodox Catholics. Then I can marry and be a priest too."

"Have your cake," I said.

"I do not understand."

He said he'd slept under the maple tree in the backyard; the bats swooped down on him through the night. He was frightened, he said, not of wild creatures but simply of the dark, and of a recurring dream he had of wafting away. He asked me where I kept the scissors for cloth and I found him an old pair of shears I had been given from the dead uncle's estate. All that day, I cleaned the house, starting with the bathroom, and working my way through the bedrooms, and the rest of the house. I found a moldy bagel end under the coffee table. In fact, I had noticed this the week prior but had done nothing about it. It had disgusted me to the point of inertia.

"What was her name?" I asked him before we finished breakfast.

"Silva. It means forest."

I watched him on and off through the morning while he unbundled a swathe of grey-green fabric and lay it out in huge pieces on the lawn. He stood over it for a great long time apparently thinking before he began to cut. And when he had finished cutting his wild swoops of curved canvas, he sat cross-legged and sewed. There was a wonderful industrial sewing machine in one of the outbuildings but I was not certain it worked and besides he was so intent, it seemed a pity to interrupt. Joshu would say later I was cruel. No, he said I was mean, but as it was self-evident that he liked this, and viewed it as a quality, I couldn't take him seriously. I am mean, I thought. Better to be mean, than average.

André came in only once, for a cup of coffee and an open-faced sandwich. I explained to him that I would be driving into the village soon, to fetch my mail at the post office and did he want anything sent out. His eyes widened and he went to his rucksack and pulled out a packet wrapped messily in brown paper. It was addressed to an S. Fraterman, of Bergensberg Plein, Ghent.

"Your lover."

"My ex-lover," he said, and looked into my eyes in a way I couldn't help but feel might be meaningful. Whatever meaningful meant or felt like, I wasn't sure I even knew.

I took the packet, placed it beside me in the car. I left Magda with André, settling her on a sheepskin over near his work. Her fat arms and legs crawled at the sky and she gurgled in that way that small babies will when they are content. "If she wails," I said, "don't worry. I'll be right back."

It was sand roads, past ghost farms the whole way. No one lived on this concession but a few hideaway eccentrics, and us. No hydro. No phone. I was thinking how the Franco-Ontarian post mistress wouldn't like the packing job André had done, and how she would tape it up and ask what it held, thinking how I would say lingerie just for her expression, when a speck up ahead in the middle of the road slowly revealed itself to be a kitten. Black, naturally.

"Holy shit." I said, and slowed to a near stop. The kitten kept coming toward the car. It moved with a slinky purpose even if it was so thin and scabby it was a wonder it lived. I thought, 'Distemper,' and then, 'Rabies.' But the truth is I hadn't a clue what was the matter with it. It came on so close to the car, I was forced to stop and wait. It circled the front tire and went under the chassis. I watched in the rearview mirror for a long time in the hope it would exit but when it did not, I got out and crouched down, looking for it.

"Kitty," I said. I felt foolish rubbing my fingers together the way people do to get the attention of small animals. "Kitty?" The kitten was curled like a monarch caterpillar on the inside of the driver wheel tire, purring. I could have reached in and pulled it out if I didn't have concerns about disease, and simply being bitten. "Come, kitty." If I drove off, I would crush it, and I didn't feel prepared for that. With a stick, I drew a line from its front paws to the edge of the road, where tussocks of plantain grew. I hoped to entice it with the movement of the stick, or the line itself, hopes that were dashed when the kitten gave a thin meow and rolled over onto its back.

"Damn you, kitten," I said. I would have to walk, then. I leaned into the car and grabbed André's packet. It took me an hour to the village and another to walk back. I endured the glare of the postmistress, smiled as she wound wide, clear tape around and around the package.

"C'est quoi ca?"

"Toile." She wrote this carefully on the packing slip, and placed André's package in the outgoing bin.

"Bien," she said and nodded good-day to me.

The kitten was gone when I reached the car; I checked each wheel. A black kitten was no omen, I decided, was more of a blessing. I turned the car and made it home quickly, expecting

Magda to be beside herself. She was wrapped in a beach towel that André had rigged around himself into a kind if papoose and was fast asleep.

"Some of the Spanish peasants wore their babies like this." He was smiling. "And look! I have finished my tent."

It lay in a heap under the maple. "Will it work?" I asked. "Is it waterproof?"

"I leave tomorrow. Take the baby," he said. "I will show you."

The wind was moving from the north, had turned cooler and swifter. I held Magda, considered the dead weight of sleep, considered how I did not want things to change. I thought how I did not love him like a lover, or a priest, but that he reminded me of something important, and while I thought, I watched him leverage the heavy cloth and whip it loose from itself. His arm muscles shone, and I worried Joshu might at any minute arrive home, and spoil this. The canvas caught air beneath it. It ballooned and opened into an oblong dome, frightful juts where it had been inexpertly sewn.

"André, hold on!" I said, and he did, was straining to keep the tent grounded. It lifted him, but only for a split second. "I float," he said, as it pulled him up a second time, feet hovering like magic.

I could see he was frightened. Magda woke up then and began first to fuss and then to scream. "Jiggle her," he suggested, as the wind pulled at the cloth, so that it whipped and struggled, cracking loudly. Magda wailed so hard I almost did not hear the canvas finally strain and begin its long, strangled rip. The cloth breathed once and then deflated, a long, devastating tear appearing down one seam and into the uncut bias.

"You will mend it," I said. He was already crying, though, curling into himself and gathering the tent up to his body. "It is only cloth," I said. "It can easily be repaired."

Michael V Smith

WOLF LAKE

It was down that road I brought her, still
in the trunk of my car. The late September
sun continued to burn, my skin slick
with sweat and dusted with the grit
of the road. In the back window, the drone
of a horsefly desperate to get out, wings small
dull chainsaws against the glass. I was eager
to be rid of the noise. There are sounds
I cannot forget. Her clucking as I carried her
over the brittle, yellow grass, steel against
wetted bone, our huffy breathing like lovers
after a vigorous dance. I say the apartment did it.
By the end of summer, I could hear everything
which living alone provides – the kitchen knives
asleep in the drawer, the sunken couch, even
the carpet lonely for something more than my
two dumb feet. Some moods are so black
they move backwards. We never loved
the campgrounds and lake, clear nights
passing a spliff at the beach. Don't be fooled.
The world can be taken from us more easily
than we from it. I learned it's hard
to kill a girl. You've got to cut her deep
and you've got to cut her right and I had done
neither. Nothing about that night was easy.
I loved my Chrysler and knew there would
be blood. Unlocking the trunk, my guts roiled
for what was next. Months of thinking
came down to this, my future and my past

bound in the moment, waiting for release
to be it's own pleasure. Hell yes, I've lived
to recognize the cage, each of us born to serve
desire, to suckle life and spit it up, hungry,
unsatisfied. Let's not be fools. Take all
you can. The crows on my back lawn
which made a sparrow a meal taught me
after death a girl is no less a girl, nor less
valuable. Animals, like God, love all things,
the living and the dead, equally. Only we
have a word for corpse. Still, you ask question
after question, struggling to uncover why,
which could be answered if you had any interest
in how. Her hands spooned like lovers tied
behind her back and her clothes sequined
with blood. Finally, she looked me in the eye
as a pickup rounded the corner and I knew
I would lose her. Her body wet and limp
over my shoulder as the truck fishtailed
to a stop. She was too much. I dropped her
and ran for the trees. The second shot
hit my shoulder and bone lodged in my eye.
I fell. I tasted what I thought must be
somebody else's blood, and the woods.

Andrew Daley

THE SLIDE

MY FATHER DISAPPEARED first, mere months after my birth. He left his job as a high school vice-principal, his wife, his daughter – that's me – and, lucky for us, a post-war bungalow on the ice-encrusted outskirts of Ottawa. Thanks to the hard work of my mother, things were much less desperate than they could have been.

Mine was the next departure. Armed with a degree in languages I went to Spain, where I taught English for a year to kids not much younger than myself. I had romantic notions of living off sangria and seafood, and that a beautiful Spanish man – so unlike the pale, well-meaning, but oafish boys in Ottawa – would fall in love with me. Instead I quartered with three girls to a room in a concrete suburb of Madrid. I traveled a bit at the end of the school term, but was anxious to get home.

There I found my mother had replaced me. Lindy, three years my junior, was the daughter of a friend of my mother's who'd withdrawn to an artists' colony on distant Vancouver Island. My mother had given Lindy my bedroom, transferring my few belongings and clothes to the basement. I wasn't unwelcome at home. It was just that, in my absence, my mother had discovered that she wasn't finished with mothering.

Lindy hoped to attend Carleton University for journalism, and shared my mother's enthusiasm for the gingham and lace country crafts gradually engulfing the house. Seven years later, Lindy was still there and still planning to study one thing or another. I got the more expensive gifts on the few Christmases I visited, but my mother's gifts to Lindy demonstrated an interest in her boarder that she no longer had in her daughter.

I moved to Toronto, where I waitressed while I interned at a hip, downtown television station. A few days of filling in for an ill meteorologist led to a contract position as something called a Weather Specialist. My appearance received an enthusiastic response, particularly from male viewers, and I enjoyed buoyancy and a momentum I'd never know before.

Greg was a handsome and polite, though pale, man in the accounting department. We dated for three years. Two months after he got a better-paying job at a rival station he asked me to marry him. There was no good reason to refuse him, and we purchased a small house just to the west of High Park.

I called the weather on the 11:00 news the night The Slide began: rain, heavy at times, possibly mixed with wet flurries north of the city. I did not predict freezing rain. In my analysis of the data, compiled for me by a real meteorologist, the spring-like warm air masses cycling in from the American Midwest made freezing rain an impossibility.

I was wrong. The rain froze as it settled onto the earth. It wasn't a major ice storm. There were no fatalities associated with it. Although it inconvenienced many people it was no doubt forgotten as soon as it was over.

That night, I recall thinking that traffic along The Queensway was oddly heavy for 12:30 a.m. I remember talking on my cell to Greg about a retirement party for his father. I remember approaching the intersection of The Queensway and Windermere Avenue.

Just as plainly, I remember my Jetta suddenly sliding sideways – this is why I call it The Slide – creating a stomach-dropping sensation of weightlessness that's still ongoing. I remember reaching for my purse, which was flying into the backseat, and the coffee mug where I kept loose change for parking. I looked up in time to see headlights boring down on me.

Head injuries are peculiar. I might have wound up quadriplegic. I might have died. Instead I spent three months in St. Joe's fighting through what felt like a perpetual fog of impatience. I didn't care that I'd lost some peripheral vision. I needed to get back on the air. Baffled doctors called it a concussion, and discharged me when they were no longer able to find anything physically wrong with me.

Other changes soon became apparent. I could no longer stand citrus fruit, or bullshit of any sort. Even the smallest crowds terrified me, and I'd become hyper – or manically, according to Greg – organized in planning my day. Also, I no longer wanted to be married.

Worse, in my absence from the station a new meteorologist was found. The replacement Weather Specialist was replaced. Management offered me a position producing entertainment segments. I lasted a month because I couldn't abide other peoples' – particularly teenaged pop stars' – tardiness or any deviations from my rigid daily timetable.

The mother of a colleague got me a job at a bank, where I perfunctorily filled or rejected health insurance claims, depending on rules set down in various employers' contracts, for a predetermined number of hours every day. My divorce from Greg, underway at this time, wasn't quite so black and white.

My waning, minor celebrity shadowed me. Strangers stopped me to ask where I'd gone, why I'd left, or what looked different about me (my nose had been broken). The more this occurred, the more determined I became to work in front of the cameras again. Sadly, jobs like those were rare, and my nose was less attractive than I was willing to admit.

One Sunday, when I called my mother for our monthly chat, I was informed that her number was no longer in service. Eventually I got a neighbour on the phone, and learned that my mother, and Lindy, had sold the house for an RV and hadn't been seen for a few weeks. Gone to look for my father, perhaps. I'm glad I never learned the true nature of that relationship.

More personality quirks surfaced. I'd gone from unflappable to easily excitable. I'd also developed an annoying habit of interrupting people when they were speaking. And – known only to me – I'd lost the French and Spanish for which I'd studied so hard, and some days could barely speak English. I'd become, as well, far less discriminating in my men, and had made some choices that would have disgusted the earlier me.

By this point it was clear that The Slide was still underway. Nonetheless, I believed that all would be restored if I could just call the weather again.

Nearly a year after my accident I heard that a cable station in a town called Summerland near Niagara Falls needed someone to call their weather. My interview was farcical. I could barely remember my name. This was why I was extremely surprised, two days later, to receive an offer to work as an administrative assistant at the station.

With little more than a slow death at the bank and dull nights-out-with-the-girls to look forward to in Toronto, I did a disappearing act of my own from my apartment, and was in Summerland, ready to work, two days later. First runner-up weathergirl is okay for now.

I rent a small house quite like the one in which I grew up that's not far from the station. I had a ridiculous affair with the man who hired me, which I suppose was what he was after, but now spend much of my free time alone. Summerland gets less snow that Ottawa, but is otherwise indistinguishable from my hometown.

The alternative – if I hadn't wrecked my Jetta – is that I'd be alone wrangling two or three kids under five in a huge house in the suburbs. Now I own a four-wheel-drive Jeep.

• • •

IF EVER I wonder if I've done something to deserve this, or if I might have worked things out otherwise, I practice calling the weather in front of my bathroom mirror. Sometimes I use a hairbrush for a microphone, like I did when I was seven-years-old and pretending to sing like Bonnie Tyler.

I predict ... unpredictability. Snow, mixed with rain. There will come a day when an icy sidewalk will flip you onto your behind. There will also be occasional days of sunshine.

Sharon McCartney

AGAINST COYOTES

Bushrats ambush unaware housecats, snipers
reconnoiter their Leningrad of suburban sagebrush,
asphalt and gravel, their alto bagatelles infiltrate
late night TV. One worms into my sister's skull,
scratches up a bed of ganglia and whelps a malign
brood there. Another screws me behind the house,
gets me stoned first, then lifts my shirt, lipsticks
my nipples with foam from the creases of his chops.
One dogs my Joan of Arc mother, dragging a leg,
aping her pathos, her someday-my-prince-will-come.
I hate that one. As I do the one who shoots craps
in Vegas with my father, claws clotted with caked-
on lies, snores with him in a parking lot off the strip,
both of them infinitely more at ease in the casino's
cornucopia of tedium, oddballs, than they are at home.
One's here with me now, arthritic, his calcified bones
buckled in the warmth of a folded afghan, sorrow's
psychedelia tickling his siesta. I stroke his skinny
ruff and he shivers with pleasure, his mulligrubs
vanquished, as if he had given discontent a smooch
and a hug, hailed a cab for it, pitiless, turning away.
This one I suffer unto me. With a dagger, I open
his belly, curl into the vaginal grasp of its cavity
and shelter there, sheathed in repudiation's regimentals.

DOROTHY

Forget the heart, I tell him. *What you've got
is way better.* I fancy the mettle of his metal
between my thighs, red poll of his hatchet
raised high. Nail me in a field of poppies!
Bend me over the emerald throne! *Why
don't we do it in the yellow brick road?*
I croon. We ditch Mr. Scarecrow with
his itch-inducing scruples, picking straws,
and yap-happy Toto won't be watching
me and my tap-dancing point man, retooled
Sherman tank clanking me to the ground
where we strip and screw, out of our minds
in the fuscous shadows behind the shack,
panting on a bed of tarnished leaves, twigs
ratcheting – Oh he has all I ever imagined,
implements, lubricants, and the inclination
to use them, a deviant tilt. I oil him and he
oils me, hot as a blowtorch under my seersucker,
his tongue a silvery soldering iron, welding
animal to mineral, my mouth grazing his nuts
and bolts. To hell with Kansas, Aunt Em,
gingham. I want to stay with him – to be his.
But he's cool under his tin lid, zippers up
and scoots. To him, it was sport – to me,
salvation. As the balloon wafts, as the munchkins
cavort, as the Wizard faretheewells, I feel
the first stain of rust, my heart's oxidation.

Goran Simic

THE AFTERLIFE OF SUICIDES

When Tito was transferred to our Homicide Dept none of us in the Antwerp police force was overjoyed. We talked behind his back, watching him sitting at his desk and reading medical books: just one more lazy young detective fired by the Brussels police. He was always swallowing some kind of pill. When we learned that he was terminally ill with cancer, we stopped dragging him to murder investigations and left him to occupy himself with suicide cases. He was perfect at it. Whenever someone reported a suicide, the colour would return to his grey face. He never waited for orders but sped to the suicide scene. For the most part, the suicides were immigrants with difficulties adjusting to their new life. I would watch Tito, with a smile on his face, writing his report, and could never get over how anyone could enjoy concerning himself with someone else's failed life.

Some years later they suddenly retired me. They didn't mention that I had neglected the Suicide Dept and for years had failed to notice how Tito's reports never included suicide notes. I should have guessed. Tito came to my office even before I managed to gather from my desk drawer the few gifts that I received at my hastily arranged retirement party. He cried and thanked me for not firing him a long time ago. I knew he was hiding the suicide notes. He told me that comparing the notes had revealed to him the secret to eternal life and that I would be the first person to whom he passed it on. Before he died.

Who knows why I believed him? Maybe because I had noticed that he had stopped taking pills and was reading medical journals with an enigmatic smile on his face. In the meantime I lived my life as patiently as a plant and waited for Tito to call.

Then I died. I simply forgot to breathe waiting for him to call me. As I was leaving, I saw Tito enter my house and rummage through my desk drawers. Obviously, he was looking for my suicide note. I listened to him telling his new boss how close he was to discovering the secret of eternal life.

Life is always like this. We are always one step away from a big secret. And then we suddenly die.

SPEECH WRITER

When the Cattlemen's Party of Sierra Leone won the election, the only thing they inherited in the devastated Parliament building was Tito, the President's speech writer. They wished they could hang him, along with the old President, except that he was the only person able to extract sweet nectar from poisoned words.

They inherited him, to put it simply, in the same manner they inherited the empty state coffers.

He liked money and his body was bent in such a way that it looked like he was crawling instead of walking. He had already written a speech for the new President in which the old government was accused of burning fields of grass.

As the new President read his speech to the suspicious cattlemen, Tito was the first one to applaud him.

The next year, when the Party of Foresters took over the State palace, Tito had in his hand a speech written for the new President in which the former government was accused of setting forests on fire and causing Great Famine. And guess who was the first to get up and applaud at the end of the speech? Tito was also the first to rejoice at the hanging of the old President.

The same happened when later on the Army of Poor Farmers entered the Palace, knowing that the only way out was with a rope around one's neck. The new President, who was literate enough to read only beer labels, didn't hide his pleasure in addressing the drunken crowd. And nobody noticed that he was just repeating words that Tito was feeding him as he hid behind the curtain. He didn't doubt for even one moment that the speechwriter would be he first one to applaud him when he announced the hanging of the old President.

Who knows how long Tito would have lasted if the Students' Party had not taken over the Palace. Instead of bearing rifles, they came armed only with pencils, and without a need to follow the old tradition of hanging. That was the first time that Tito sat in the audience without applauding. His hands were crumpling newly written speeches that nobody paid attention to. Later, even his old allies, cleaning ladies, cooks and flag designers, stopped caring for his complaints, and one day he opened the back door of the Palace and left.

They were watching him from the windows as he skipped over the graves of former presidents, then over the decaying cows and the fields of hunger, and then vanished towards the burnt forest.

"Why is he applauding to himself?" thought the cleaning lady.

"And why does he have a rope around his neck?" thought the new President.

Emily Shultz

I LOVE YOU, PRETTY PUPPY

I'M IN LOVE with you and the dog is licking herself.

That's my life.

We lay on the bed, our smell rising up in the steam heat of this dismal apartment, our ugly skin the best part of our lives together: your arm under my head, and my ugly face turned into the small perfect heartbeat that taps out of your sunken chest. Our naked legs tangle together in a spidery imitation of hair and skin. Our fluids dry all sweet and sour, yours in mine and mine on yours. And I love you. I love you from the only beautiful part of me, the part that neither of us can see.

On the floor next to the bed, the dog has stopped scratching, stopped shaking the room with the thwack of her leg and the jangle of tags. Instead, she's started licking the place between her legs. Making the room sound like rain. And it's gross, like us, this inappropriate lapping.

"O.K., get off," you say, squirming out from underneath me. Rolling up off the mattress, your body falls around you again, like a bird spreading its wings. Your ass is like a sponge that has sopped up something heavy. A sprinkle of acne scars your shoulders. These are the leftovers of adolescence as we pull up into our thirties. You drift away from me.

You walk out of the room slowly, and in the light of the bathroom doorway, you push your hair out of your eyes. In silhouette, you could be graceful, if I didn't know you the way that I do. If I didn't know.

I put my hand between my legs and feel the place where we meet. It's sticky.

In the other room, the pipes whistle. You run the water, and as you wait for it to warm – though I can't see you – I know you are standing over the toilet, pissing.

• • •

IT'S TERRIBLE REALLY, to live this way. The first time I saw
you, I fell in love with you. I knew at that exact moment that
– for better or worse – we would be together forever. Until
that day I had never seen anyone uglier than me. Or at least,
no one who hadn't been deformed by some birth defect or
accident. No one who had been marred by a simple meeting
of bad genetics coming to the forefront without any nameable
disability. Do you know what it means to feel that way? You
do, I know you do, but it still makes me self-consciously sick
inside. My whole life, the only time I felt good about myself
was when I saw someone less fortunate than I was.

I tried to be good. I was good. But then it would creep up,
every once in a while, when I was lucky, when I was unlucky.
It would be there, like the boy at the back of the bus who wore
puppy dog sweaters when we were in the eighth grade, their
blotchy blue yarn snouts and banana-shaped ears stitched
onto the pockets.

He was my salvation. Him, and the rare – the few – others
like him. He tried to speak to me, to make friends, but I never
let him. We were alike, but not. After all, he wasn't really ugly,
just faultlessly stupid. After a while, our silence became spe-
cial. It stretched from front to back, over the seats, an invisible
cloud of love and hate. I could feel him staring at the back of
my head. The wind blew my hair all around, making a wild
nest that I tried and tried to keep down. Sometimes I would
gaze up into the large rectangle of the driver's rear-view. I
would catch him staring; he was too dim to realize I could
see him in the reflection. His mouth was slack, his eyes sad. I
did love him. I did, in a way. I imagined that he drank milk at
night, that his mother still brought it to him in bed and kissed

him, that he dreamt Disney characters would come and help him capture all of the smart, beautiful, normal kids and send them away. That one day he and I would meet on the Island of Misfit Toys. But we shared only that – silence and a few angry glances – a secret attraction and aversion I controlled cruelly. Ignoring him was worse than anything the other kids could do to him.

Thankfully, by the time I met you, I was old enough to know better. Old enough to have developed self-interest, a strange, disjointed, macabre fascination with myself. Not narcissism – they say that that word is always misused – but you know what I mean. I'm sure you know the word for it, even though I don't.

No, by then, ugliness had become a kind of light to me. I had grown used to it, had even learned to look for it.

In my last year of high school, I developed an enormous crush on the fat girl who brought her father as her date to the prom. She was stronger than I was. She had a satin fuchsia dress. She at least had someone to dance with. She didn't care what they thought. I had only the girl with the harelip who got straight A's and talked to me about mathematics, as if that could be considered conversation. We huddled together, daring one another to down the spiked punch, poking one another in the ribs, saying no when one of the hockey guys ambled over and asked her – then me – to dance. We were wise and gutless. It was only a joke. And on the way home, we vomited up peach schnapps behind the Mac's convenience and confessed we each wished we'd said yes, even if we knew he would go back to his friends to collect bet money. To feel for just three minutes his taut body holding us tentatively, above our heads his bright skin, his velvet cheeks, his valentine lips, his eyes like plums. Why do I still remember?

The girl in the fuchsia dress became a journalist. The harelip girl became a professor of mathematics. The boy with the liquid eyes knocked up his girlfriend and then left her. He became manager at a McDonald's. He stopped playing hockey, balded early, got fat.

Scenarios like this helped me to survive. Kept me from locking myself in the bathroom, holding my father's razor like a crucifix.

When I was still an adolescent, they told me they could fix my face. Part of it, anyway. One night, after my parents had gone to sleep, I got up and, in the orange glow of the night light; I stood staring into the mirror – for over an hour. Looking in turn at the different features of my face. My eyes. My nose. My jaw. My mouth. Coming back to my eyes again. I said to myself, "This is my face." To change any one part of it would change the entire thing.

"This is my face," I said.

• • •

I MET YOU in a crowded room, everyone talking, someone passing around a sweet-burning paper cone full of pot. People were dancing in the foot or two of space between the living room and kitchen of this little apartment. And then there was you, sitting in the corner, every gesture you made slow and deliberate, and everyone in the room (who wasn't dancing or stoned) looking at you, gathered around you, gradually moving chairs closer to you or sitting down on the patch of worn carpet in front of you, all of them looking and listening.

You struck me as a circus performer. You were fat-thin, your hair long-short, the fingers that held your cigarette swollen like those of a midget (though I know that's not what they like to be called). You gestured with this lit thing, gracefully, turning your head, your large round eyes, your mouth pulling open, pulling open, pulling open before the words would come out. You weren't handicapped. You weren't retarded.

You weren't even ugly. You were beautiful, the only one there who wasn't uniform. They all wore jeans and brown loafers and iron-flat buttoned shirts. You wore an oversized T-shirt and jogging pants and a pair of old runners. I couldn't take my eyes off you. And when I got closer, I could see why they all stared too. The things that fell from your mouth were unbelievable. My walking trivia box. My living history boy. My gorgeous genius.

I broke into a sweat. I knew you could never love me. Right then, just like that, my mind was made up. I would love you for all I was worth, if only you would look at me, just look at me.

When we made love the first time, it was as if we were kids in a playroom, trying not to get caught shoving plastic toys down our shorts. Your cock was like a small mouse inside me. Furry and brown, ready to leave its leg behind in a rush to get away. We made love again and again until we got better at it. Until we were like two adults in a hotel room instead. We made love until we were dirty and gasping. We were ugly, we were the ugly people, and we had no right to this. We did it again, just to be sure. Just to show them. The non-existent them we felt were more real than ourselves.

Months and months of this.

• • •

AND THEN, ONE day, me pissing and moaning about the ass-holes at work, an asshole on the bus, an asshole on the radio saying some asshole thing, people moving around not want-ing to sit next to me, some kid looking at me like I was more disgusting than a turd on a stick. Over an afternoon table, this conversation drifted above a plate of nachos, some non-descript band on the jukebox, and you said, "One day you'll look back, and think these were the best times of your life."

"I hope I would never think that these are the best times of my life."

"Yes, you will," you said. "You think you're ugly now? You're only going to get uglier."

"Well, thanks," I said. I couldn't believe you could be so cruel. "Thanks a fucking lot."

You leaned back, all confidence, the smell from your armpits hitting me gently as you stuck your palms behind your head. That tangy one-time aphrodisiac, now greasy and gross as congealed cheese.

"The same goes for me," you said. "For everyone. You should see things as they are. It's never been as bad as you think."

And then you launched into some example, or string of examples. You were a double-major in history and religion. In spite of being an atheist. You have an example for everything. But I wasn't listening. I began thinking about the differences between men and women – and how I would only grow older and uglier, but you would grow wiser – and how an unattractive man is never as undesirable as an unattractive woman, particularly if he is intelligent or distinguished in some way – and how when we do go out you are the one that people want to make conversation with – and how I will sit to the side exchanging the most menial pleasantries – how people have always clustered around you, in spite of your looks – how you are the kind of person people wait to speak to – and I am the kind they walk away from. Sometimes mid-sentence.

A giant fear began to rumble through my stomach. I knew you would leave me, knew it as certainly as I had known six years before that we would always be together. You would grow successful – you were already – and there would be women—and there would be flirtations – and they would be beautiful – and they would be open to you for the first time – and then I would not be interesting. I would just be ugly.

Uglier, even.

Were you with me because you loved me? Or because at the time I was all you could have? Did you keep me because you wanted me? Or because you just didn't have the heart to get rid of me?

That night, for the first time since I was a teenager, I locked myself in the bathroom to cry. You tried to come in, but I'd locked the door. The knob turned and stuck.

"Are you O.K., babe?" you called through the door, easy-like, the way you are.

"Go away," I said, sniffing back mucous. "I'm taking a shit."

"But you're taking so long … ?"

"Must have been something I ate," I lied. The only truth in it was that my guts felt like a needle had been put through them repeatedly, sewing them into a fist.

"The dog's desperate to go out," you said.

"Then you take her."

• • •

AT A CERTAIN point, hate goes past hate and, if not back to love again, then at least to liking. Truly attractive people had become that to me long ago. After I met you, their beauty stopped bothering me.

Until I met Norman.

It was the same as when I met you, only worse. I was completely repulsed. The idea that I would want to lay a body like mine next to a body like his sent me into cold sweats in my seat. He was flawless and beautiful, but only on one side.

He worked two cubicles over. I was grateful for the fuzzy grey half-walls between us. It meant I didn't have to look at him. His head was shocking, its short bright hair like an ad for a shampoo commercial. He had the body of a greyhound.

His shoulders were fists and his waist was abominably narrow. When he turned sideways, he was all muscle and rib cage. I had never seen anyone so conventionally perfect. But when he turned to the other side, his skin pulled away in white ridges, and he was half-skeleton, the long scars running in vertical wrinkles across his gorgeous face. His pocked neck. His twisted shoulder flesh. His hard, hollow skin. He'd been burned.

I had never been attracted to anyone like him, had never seen the circumstances of our lives being as hard as those of our birthrights. How golden his life must have been, and then to have it all yanked away, scalding ... How far down his body did those bone-like scars go? Did they diverge across his chest? Or stretch all the way over his hipbones? I wanted to feel him tear at my skin, feel his anger at the injustice, feel it manifest in the blunt, mesmerizing beat of lust.

I kept an inventory of his habits. He was polite – and frugal with himself and with others – and he was a drink-box bachelor, his lunches nothing but gym towels he hung to dry on the hook inside his cubicle – and he kept a bottle of salve inside his desk drawer – and it smelled like pine needles and eucalyptus – and, to make matters worse, a good thick novel he replaced every week with another – and he was a two-finger typist, though almost as fast as a professional – and the keys clicked underneath the clean crescent moons of his impeccable nails – and when he walked by, he moved like a cat – and he always smirked instead of fully smiling as though he was thinking something dirty – and the skin on his burned side was the colour one imagines an angel's wing would be – and around him I felt myself lift, my breasts become little pieces of lace, stitched on.

At night, you moved over me like a ghost, and I no longer felt you or smelled you. Afterward, I would walk the dog.

Out in the snow, she padded in circles, sniffing, pushing

her nose down into the ground, long strings of saliva collecting ice.

"Why can't I have this?" I asked. I whispered it out loud into the cold empty night. "This," meaning Norman, meaning something beautiful, or half-beautiful. "Just once," I thought, "why not me?"

The dog squatted and did her business.

When I came back in, you were uglier than ever.

• • •

I LOCKED MYSELF in the bathroom. I shaved my legs. I took a loofah and did my feet. I pulled hairs from my nipples with tweezers. You knew me. You knew I was ugly and you had stopped seeing my ugliness. To Norman, everything would be obvious. The hairs would jut from my body like curls of copper wire. My feet would be rough as concrete. My thighs would be soft and wrinkled as a lizard's underbelly.

• • •

NORMAN LIKED ME. No one had ever liked me before. You had loved me, but I doubted now that you had ever liked me.

"You're very interesting," he said, letting the emphasis fall on the first part of the word. Norman said I was clever. Norman said I was hilarious. Norman said I was sweet. He did not say any of the things that other people had said. He did not say, "Do you ever think of getting your teeth straightened?" or "Have you tried contact lenses?"

We went for coffee after work. It became a regular thing. We stayed out very late and never talked about work. He told me about his apartment (above a convenience store), his previous girlfriends (one shallow, another fickle), other places he had lived (the West), the places he had travelled (the East), and what he most desired (to accurately document the time we were living in). I desperately wanted to ask him how it had happened, how he had been burned, but I knew everyone else must have asked him that. For Norman it must have been the equivalent of, "Have you ever tried to do something else with your hair?"

He smiled his half-smile. He smirked, and smirked, and smirked some more. His mouth was like a faint red comma penciled on a piece of paper. It was obvious what he was thinking. We were going to have an affair. We were going to have a wonderful, awful affair. I glanced in the mirror across from our booth and I saw a man and a woman. In the dim lighting of the diner, I could not see our faults, only our profiles. "That is what she looks like," I thought to myself, "the woman who has an affair."

• • •

IN THE SHADOWS of the parking garage, Norman's car smelled like leather and oil. I thought of you, just once, as I was getting in. Then Norman's bad side was to me, and he leaned in and kissed me on the mouth. His tongue was softer than the rest of him, and that made me nervous. I pulled to the side and wound up laying my lips against his scars before I realized it. He put his hands up my shirt without asking, and then, before I realized it, he had slid them down into my lap. He moved with the fast confidence of a beautiful man, even as my mouth was pressed against his ugly part.

Up close he didn't look ugly or beautiful. He just looked like a stranger.

"I can't," I said, "I can't." I pushed him away from me.

He smelled all wrong. Like mint leaves and pine incense.

"What do you mean?" he said, and when I started to cry, he slapped the dash hard, and not with the flat part of his hand. He got out of the car and made some adjustments to his clothes. When he got back in, he revved the engine and drove too fast.

I stared into the side-view mirror all the way home. I could see part of my face in it – my mouth – my ugly mouth and the black side of this stranger's car.

Even ugly people could be assholes.

• • •

WHEN I ENTERED the apartment I could tell something had happened. Things had been thrown here and there, newspapers and a couple of cardboard boxes. Your old pair of shoes tripped me in the doorway of the bedroom. A blanket hung over the arm of the chair. A strange stale smell lingered in the air.

Everything was much too still.

Panic threw a punch at my head and I gripped the doorframe. Then I realized what exactly was so wrong: you were gone, but so was the dog.

• • •

AT THE EMERGENCY vet clinic, you slumped among a long row of plastic chairs. Above you, a television strapped to the wall played a late-night infomercial. As I came through the doors, I watched your face hanging there, blotchy, a clown's face, your expression fixed, permanent. You stood up but didn't move, and for the first time, I think, I really knew you needed me as much as I did you. I forgot what I had done an hour before and I grabbed hold of you.

"Is she all right?" I asked. I could feel fear on your skin like an extra layer. You gripped my back with your hands, your fingers spread.

On the phone message at home, you had explained the oceans of puke, and how she had crawled half under our bed – you thought – to die. The vet didn't know what was wrong with her.

A wave of your perspiration hit my face as you pulled me into your shoulder. "I'm sorry," I said, even though she was my dog, technically. Even though I had been the one crying all the way over in the taxi. Even though I was the more wretched of the two of us and didn't deserve to be anywhere – even here – with you. Your body felt bumpy and right, warm and accepting through your old grey sweatshirt.

"I love you," I said. It was all I could think of to say.

• • •

THEY LET ME go into the back to see her. The room where they had her was about the size of a bathroom, bare except for this animal tethered to an I.V.

She sprawled on her side in the middle of the floor, and didn't move when I came in. I could tell by the smell that she had let her glands go earlier. The bitter stink still streaked the air. Her back end was dirty – dirty smeared clean – as though she might have defecated on herself at some point and some intern had made a half-hearted attempt to wipe her up. I said her name, but she still didn't move. She found me with her eyes, but showed no sign of caring. Her eyes had turned yellow with jaundice. Her dark pupils floated in two small pools of pus in her long face. I had never seen anything so pathetic. She was feeble, pitiful, and sad.

I fell to my knees and put my hands in her fur, stroking the top of her head and behind her ears. "Please don't die," I whispered. "Please stay with me. Please. Stay."

Behind me, I could hear you trying not to cry.

"I love you, pretty puppy," I whispered. "My beautiful

doggy girl." I put my lips to the crest of her crusted nose and kissed her.

Catherine Graham

PIGS

Here comes that truck again about to turn down Strachan.
That transport truck full of them, trapped in aluminum crates.
I know they roll in the wet pen dirt to cool off, self-regulate,
but all I see is pink through the air holes.

I have to admit I like pork, so why the urge to hoof
out here by the Princes' Gates and stop that grunting truck?
Silent in their boxes, do they know the gore they're going to be?
It seems I've picked up on some kind of radar,
the terror with no sound the body hears without moving.

HEAVY WITHOUT HEAVY RAIN

It doesn't matter what I'm listening to as I pull
over to the wrong side of the road
to better listen before parking underground.
Radio shot when you walk by –
under an umbrella, your solid hand
on the back of a coat – blue raincoat –
your solid hand in the middle of her back
moving her forward, your long back to me.
I feel the thick of my stomach
curdle to brick, holding me there, here,
a dry anchor, a doppelgänger, seen through
rain's veil, after the funeral. Your life without me.

Moez Surani

IN TIMES OF DROUGHT

DAYS AGO, THEY walked past the ruins of two Soviet MiGs. Nooria had taken her hat off and scratched her head at the oddity of this sight in this land of mountain desert. Malik walked on, hardly glancing at the wreckage.

"Malik, when we get to Iran, what will you do?"

He doesn't look at her when he speaks. He doesn't like to see the size of her pack strapped to the back of her little body. She insists on carrying it without his help. He thinks her too proud.

"There are jobs shelling pistachios," he says. "But these are very poor. Maybe if I grow bigger I can be a construction worker. I have heard those men are paid well enough. I could shell pistachios first though."

"I can shell pistachios too."

"No, you will go to school."

"Nana said you taught me well. That I've learned to read fast and that I may be as smart as you. I can shell pistachios after school though. We can shell them together."

When Nooria walks, a spoon in her pack clanks inside an empty thermos. There are times when the distance between them can grow to thirty yards. Malik does not look back. He listens for the clanking of her spoon to know how far behind she has fallen and if he must slow his pace.

Most of the time they walk in silence. Other times they play their game.

"Elbow," she says.

Malik thinks for a moment. "White."

"What does 'White' end in?"

"E."

"E," she says to herself searching for a word. "E is difficult. You should give me words that end in S or T or R." She walks in silence canvassing the surrounding landscape for clues.

"Ear," she says in triumph.

"Rock. K."

The clanking of her spoon against metal. "K. Cup."

"Cup starts with C not K."

She looks up at him and scratches the side of her face. "Ok. K. Kid."

"Den. N."

"N," she says to herself. "What's a 'Den'?"

"It's where bears live."

"N," she says to herself imagining where bears could live. "Nooria!" she says grinning. "Nooria!"

Malik thinks for a moment. "Axe. E."

Nooria looks at Malik and shakes her head sadly. "Malik, E words are hard."

• • •

IT WAS SIX days ago when he had told Nooria to pack.

"Where are we going?" she asked.

"Iran."

"What is in Iran?"

"Elephants."

"What's an elephant?"

"An animal. I'll tell you as we walk."

Nooria jumped to her feet to pack. She had always been interested in strange animals. "Tell me about elephants!" she pleaded as she packed.

• • •

NOORIA PULLS AT Malik's elbow. "Malik, tell me about elephants."

"I have already told you all I know."

"But tell me again, Malik. I like when you show how they walk."

"Ok, Nooria. They're big. Bigger than any animal you can imagine. And they don't have noses. They have trunks that hang long, all the way to the ground. And –"

"And how do they walk, Malik? Show me how they walk."

"They have tails that swat at any flies or birds that land on their backs. Their skin is grey and wrinkly as –"

"As Bapa!"

"Wrinkly as Bapa. And they have white tusks that curl –"

"And how do they walk, Malik?"

"They have white tusks, one on each side of the trunk, that curl up to the sky." He shrugs his pack off his shoulders. "And many years ago, the leaders would sit atop the elephants." Malik kneels down so Nooria can climb onto his back. He lifts her into the air, her arms wrapped around his neck. "They would climb atop the elephants and rise into the sky." He stomps around in a circle with her on his back. "They would sit on the elephants on top of red carpets and decorate the animals so they were as royal as the people that rode on them. And the elephants would lift them above trees and temples, above the sounds of the markets and the smells of the sea. The elephants lifting them all into the sky." He kneels over so she can hop off.

"Thanks Malik!" She says, kissing him on the cheek. "Malik," she says flush with confidence, "You're my favorite brother."

"I'm your only brother."

"Yes, but still my very favorite."

They begin walking again.

"Malik, do you believe that Allah's watching us? That he's

watching us walk to Iran to see the elephants?"

Malik walks in silence. She watches, but his face betrays no emotion.

"I believe he's watching us," she says. "I believe he plays our game too. I think he knows many E words and that he laughs at me." She scratches her head under her hat. "I think he laughs at how long it takes me to think of E words."

$$\bullet\ \bullet\ \bullet$$

THE OTHER FARMERS faced a similar situation. The worst drought in thirty years choked the new crops. Less resilient grain and vegetable crops had replaced acres of once crimson-stained fields. Faced with starvation, families began eating the seeds of what was to be this year's harvest.

Malik had first heard it as an isolated incident, as a rumor occurring somewhere beyond his field of comprehension. Then a family he had known. He would not allow it to happen to Nooria. He would not allow her to be sold into marriage for three 75 Kg bags of grain like several other girls had been.

$$\bullet\ \bullet\ \bullet$$

"EMERALD," SHE SAYS.

"Dollar. R."

"Root."

"Turtle. E."

"Malik, it's not fair. You always give me E words."

She stops walking and scratches her head that is itchy under her pink hat. A deep red against the landscape of stone and parched soil catches her eye to her right. She turns and sees a poppy, smiling as she picks it up, a memory of home. A memory of the farm and family she and Malik left behind. Someone must have dropped it, she thinks. She twirls the flower between her fingers then tucks it behind her right ear. She runs to catch up to Malik, and then walks alongside him. She is happy to walk beside him, even in silence.

• • •

THERE WAS AN unsigned letter published in the Pakistani *Dawn*. It was circulated among English speakers and quickly translated into Urdu. University students felt emboldened.

> *Do not insult me*
> *By telling me the colour of the sky,*
> *The hue of the sinking sun,*
> *· The shape of mountains at the horizon,*
> *It is all blood,*
> *Mountains, sky, sinking sun.*
>
> *Do not tell me how many Afghans have perished.*
> *This use of numbers insults the individual.*
> *Do not give me European subtleties.*
> *It is all blood,*
> *Mountains, sky, sinking sun*

Nooria jumps in front of Malik and walks backwards so they face each other. "Malik, Nana says I have learned to read and write very fast. Maybe when we get to Iran I could be a poet. I don't know how to rhyme yet but you could teach me? I could write a poem for you."

Malik drops his pack from his shoulders. "What am I to do with a poem, Nooria? Can I eat a poem? Can I sleep under it at night? What is this?" He snaps the poppy from behind her right ear, tears it apart and throws the ruined flower away to his left. He picks his pack up and walks past Nooria, brushing roughly against her. "Poems are written by rich Englishmen."

Malik hears the clanking of her spoon far behind him. A faint hint of her existence. He slows his pace so she can catch up. He has learned that she becomes sad when the distance between them grows too large. He never looks back. He worries sometimes that she may be crying.

She feels a loneliness that he does not understand. He can walk and think of nothing but the beat of his feet over the terrain. All she thinks of is what she has said to upset him. That he could be happier walking by himself without her to anger him. She wonders if he will one day walk so fast that he escapes her over the horizon. How will I get to Iran, she thinks. How will I see the elephants?

She had once heard people talking about an animal called a lion. As she listened, she thought there lived some quality of lion in Malik.

• • •

THEY ARRIVED AT the Maslaq refugee camp in western Afghanistan. They walked in the darkness towards the tents. A woman outside plunges her clothes into a bucket of water, scrubbing dirt and sand free from the fabric. A man coughs in a nearby tent. The kerosene bottle functioning as a makeshift lamp dangles from the hanging twine. And the wind lifts sand into the air, showering the grains against the plastic skin of the tent.

Malik is always the first to fall asleep. Nooria lies next to him, under their shared blanket, listening. Even when he is asleep she feels comfort in being next to him. A man in their tent had begun muttering in his sleep nights ago and Nooria had squeezed Malik's arm. She was surprised, but happy, that he did not wake. She did not wish to wake him from the land of his dreams. She lies next to him, her little hands gripping the thin muscles of his arm.

Maslaq camp where 600 Afghan refugees arrive daily to escape draught, famine, the detritus of war. Where in a span of three nights 150 people froze to death as the temperature slipped below -25 degrees Celsius.

From the January 2nd *Dawn*.

> *Do not insult me by describing the splendor of the*
>   *afterlife,*
> *Of the ethereal gardens of heaven,*
> *Do not tell me that the meek shall then attain justice,*
> *It is all blood*
> *Mountains, sky, sinking sun.*

Nooria climbs in against Malik under their shared blanket. She lies against him, listening to his slow breathing. "Elephants," she whispers to herself. "Elephant!" She shakes Malik awake. "Elephant!"

"What?"

"You said 'Turtle, E' so I say Elephant!"

Malik leans forehead and kisses her on the forehead. "Go to sleep."

Three pieces of coal glow orange in the mud floor. The riotous wind pulls at the plastic sheeting that protects them, tears at the sands, at the exposed flesh of anyone outside in the camp.

"Elephants," she whispers.

Molly Peacock

MARRIAGE

I watch my husband at a party,
a shy boy become a man at ease at last.
Success freshens his face, the boy now free
to pass beneath his expressions
as if slipping under a fence.
I used to slip under a fence
to swim in a stream-fed pond
and laze in the water till shocked
and delighted by a cold spot I swam through.
That's what his face is like,
infused by a source inside him.
I know I have a part in it,
just as I was part of the pond
where I loved to swim.

WARRIOR POSE

Blades fly from our arms in yoga class,
fingers vibrating from the stretch.
But are we ready?
Even though the blades are imaginary,
they throw us off balance, and we are less
brave warriors than if we stayed on the couch,
curled up balls, unprepared.
How can we think ourselves into the full bloom
of power and preparation? Perhaps
by imagining buds curled in our palms,
opened by the ants of persistence
and fed by new focus into peony flowers,
huge, magenta and smothering our enemy's
surprised face with lunging beauty.

Jessica Westhead

GAR'S MARINE PALACE

On Glenda's first visit to Gar's Marine Palace, Gar had fashioned a crude wedding scene with his mackerel.

"That's a good one," said Glenda's father.

"Thanks," said Gar. "You see what the ring bearer's got?"

They leaned in for a closer look.

"Calamari," said Glenda's father. "Nice touch."

Gar was a grey-cheeked and bloodless fishmonger who liked to get creative with his seafood displays.

Glenda's father turned back to Gar, but Glenda kept staring at the refrigerated tableau.

Gar's bride and groom faced each other, eyes wide open and staring, poised for a scaly nuptial kiss.

"Can fish really get married?" said Glenda.

Gar regarded her with watery, half-lidded eyes. "Why don't you take a gander at my lobster tank over there, sweetheart?"

"All right."

The tank loomed behind them. Glenda pressed her forehead against the cool glass and tapped her finger at the lobsters. She watched the reflection of the two men at the counter.

"Wrap me up four pounds of pike there, Gar."

"You got it. Caught a few of these bastards myself last weekend up at the cottage."

"That so."

Gar's pale fingers slid around one of the long, angry-looking fish. "This one here, Christ-hell-almighty, did he put up a fight! Took me near a whole half hour to reel in this son of a whore. And then I finally land him, and he goes flopping all over the boat, you know, and damned if he didn't take a chunk out of my thumb before I brained the bastard. I felt like that Captain Nemo, you know, when he harpoons that whale's dick?" Gar slapped his conquest onto the scales. "There you go. Four pounds of mean and ugly, my friend."

"Why aren't your lobsters red?" said Glenda. "Lobsters in pictures are always red."

"What? Oh. Well, that's because they're not dead yet, sweetheart. They only turn red when they're boiled."

Glenda frowned, and noticed something else. "Why do they have rubber bands around their claws?"

"That's so they don't pinch your nose off when you stick them in the pot!"

The brown lobsters—there were seven of them—marched clumsily around a slimy-looking treasure chest, with a mermaid lounging on top.

Glenda turned to look at Gar. "You mean you boil them alive?"

"That's right. And if you get real close when they're cooking you can hear them scream."

The men laughed together.

Gar leaned forward. "You like my lobsters there?"

"They're nice," said Glenda.

"You like fish?"

"Not to eat," she said.

"What about penguins?" said her father. "Penguins eat fish."

"Not *this* penguin."

Her father raised an eyebrow at Gar. "Glenda's going to be a penguin in her school play tonight."

"Is that right?" said Gar. "Well, you better start liking fish quick, then."

"I'm a vegetarian," she said.

The fish-seller snorted. "Who ever heard of a vegetarian penguin?"

Glenda ignored him. One of the lobsters was trying to get her attention.

"Penguins have to eat fish or they die. You don't want to die, do you?"

The second-biggest lobster was waving at her with its claws, in those tight elastic bands.

"Let's go, Glenda," said her father.

"Can we get a lobster?" she said.

"Why do you want a lobster? You just said you don't like fish."

"Lobsters are different. I said the lobsters were nice."

"No lobster. Let's go."

"I think she wants it for a pet," said Gar.

"Oh yeah?" Her father grinned. "You want it for a pet?"

"Maybe," said Glenda.

"Told you," said Gar.

Glenda listened to the two men laugh at the idea of a pet lobster.

"Well, I'll see you," her father said to Gar.

"See you."

"Come on, Glenda. Say goodbye." Her father reached for her hand but she pulled it away.

"Goodbye," she said to the lobsters.

• • •

THE PLAY WAS called "Floe Woes." Glenda's Drama teacher had made up the title; the rest was supposed to be improvised.

The penguin head was hot and stuffy, and Glenda couldn't see anything out of the eye-holes. She could dimly sense the action happening around her, but all she could do was stand there and sweat.

"Oh, boohoo!" she heard Jeremy the Killer Whale say. "There are no penguins and I am so hungry!"

Sasha the Sea Lion said her line next. "I am hungry too, and I also like to eat penguins!"

Glenda stayed where she was. She listened to her own amplified breathing, and then she heard her father in the audience.

"Why doesn't she *move*?" he said.

"Be quiet!" said her mother.

"She's just standing there!"

Her arms were pinned down – "Strap the wings to the sides," her Home Ec teacher had said when Glenda was making her costume in class. "Penguins don't flap."

Someone gave Glenda a shove. She shuffled forward and bumped into something.

"Yum! Penguin!" Jeremy and Sasha said together, and then the two of them fell upon her.

Glenda wasn't allowed to remove the head to take a bow at the end.

"You're the penguin," the Drama teacher said, but only so she could hear. "The *penguin* deserves the applause – you didn't do anything special."

Glenda felt bruises starting.

"Bet you're hungry for some fish *now*!" she heard her father yell.

• • •

THE NEXT TIME she saw Gar he didn't have any pickerel.

"No pickerel," he told her father. "Don't get me started on that. I told my pickerel supplier, 'If you'll do it right, then fine. If you won't, then curl up and die in a hole and make room for someone who will.' That's what I told him."

Glenda's father nodded. "You need what you need when you need it."

"That's right. So I should have pickerel by next week. I

thought you liked the pike, though."

"I do. The wife likes the pickerel."

Gar nodded. "It's a woman's fish."

Glenda was looking at Gar's display case.

"You like that?" he said. "That's my take on the Nativity."

"Is that right?" Glenda's father bent down and peered in.

"I figured it'll be Christmas in a few months, might as well be seasonal."

Glenda blinked at the assembly of fish parts that Gar had decorated with tinsel.

"That's baby squids for the Three Wise Men, and I used a tuna head for Mary."

"She's all dressed up," said Glenda's father. "Classy."

"All I put was some netting and a couple hooks for her gown. Easy. And I got a tiger shrimp there for the Baby Jesus."

"Hey, tiger shrimp." Her father straightened up. "Can I get a pound of those?"

"Sure thing."

"And I'll take some pike too."

"You got it."

Glenda walked over to the lobster tank. "Hello lobsters," she said.

"You get the pike at the cottage again?" said her father.

"Nah, not these ones. Me and Sheila went up to the Kawarthas and stayed in this Christian Fundamentalist Bed and Breakfast," said Gar. "If you know what I mean."

"Oh yeah?"

"Yeah. Not much of the you-know-what going on. The lady who ran it made good pancakes, though. I think she was one of those Ay-mish."

"I hear they're supposed to be good cooks."

"Well, the pancakes were pretty all right, I can tell you."

"I know what it's like," Glenda whispered to the lobsters.

"What's she saying over there?" said Gar.

"She's talking to your lobsters."

"Hey, you talking to my lobsters over there?"

Glenda didn't answer him.

"Hey, how'd your play go?" he said. "How was it being a penguin?"

"Fine," she said.

"She didn't move," said her father. "She just stood there."

"She get stage fright?"

"I don't know."

"You get stage fright?" Gar said to Glenda.

"No."

The lobsters looked sadder than ever. They weren't even waving this time.

Glenda tapped the glass. "There were more," she said to Gar.

"What's that?"

"You had more lobsters last time, I counted."

"You're pretty smart," he said.

"You sell some?" said Glenda's father.

"Sold a couple last week," said Gar. "I got to restock."

"How's your lobster guy?"

"Better than my pickerel guy, I'll say that much."

Glenda put her palm against the tank. The lobsters didn't move. "I'm sorry," she said.

"What'd she say?"

"I missed it," said her father. "Can you make that two pounds of the shrimp?"

"Coming right up," said Gar.

Sue Sinclair

OLD MIRRORS

Moodily we admire ourselves
in their wintry halos, the light eroded
at the edges. Where it's thinnest,
the past creeps in; curious faces
gawk at you, crowd around
your image. The useless currency
of their gaze, copper coins.
Turn your head, they disappear;
only when you look straight ahead
do they creep into the periphery.
They stare, they fill their empty coffers
with your image: you appear
as sped-up footage of their own past,
an adrenalin-induced photogenic blur,
the opposite of their dragged-out afterlives.
They would steal your soul if they could;
envy makes the light a little jaundiced
around the edges, tinged with longing.
Then something calls them away: a shadow
over your left shoulder, a whisper,
the curtain they've lifted to peer at you
falling back into place.
You turn away, bewildered,
as though a sea had parted
in the room that mere seconds ago
was empty.

SAME OLD LIGHT

The lake's reflection rippling
on the undersides
   of willows, faintly,
like a film running,
running through characters
and plot,
playing itself out, blurry,
indistinct –

it's happening, though
you can't say what it
is – the feathered antennae
of the goldenrod quiver –

Ray Hsu

HERE IS THE DISAPPOINTMENT

we call language. Bent over the stove
it is what I use as you hold the wood
spoon for me. Metal scuffs
decades of pots we've honoured.
I am now scalded. I apologize,
feign grace. In another time
I would have taken
sacrifices less for granted. I am patient,
I think. You stand up to answer
the phone, to change
the channel. Life as usual. We know each other
through these.

MARCO. POLO.

When he swaggers in on the hoar frost
it's bible and brine,
doctor. Not a fleck of dust to unwind.
He gives you this badge and you scour
your arm and no the badge won't go. It's loudest
in sunlight. It speaks to you like an urgent
outpost.

When he comes in, it's on a horse overflowing
with singing coins. Like a fountain or a silver hook,
he summons you, redeems
this valley dwelling
deep in your nature. All it takes is a good
saw.

When the smoke clears, he's fallen from the sky
to become the backdrop you carry
until you have a use for things until
you're dumb with a sadness until
you're so mighty
thankful.

James Grainger

ALL THIS IN FRONT OF THE CHILDREN, CHAPTER ONE

PITCHING HER VOICE just below the flat noise of the AM radio Liz finally finds the right simile. "Joseph," she says, "sex with Dan was like walking through an orange grove on a summer morning and reaching up and picking the sweetest, ripest orange – and it's still warm from the sun. You hold that beautiful orange in your hand and then someone offers you a glass of Tang: which one are you going to choose?"

She wants an actual answer. She needs to hear him say the orange so he does.

"After sex with Dan I never wanted Tang again. I stopped being promiscuous because I knew what sex was for."

Promiscuity was drinking glass after glass of Tang and still being thirsty; good sex the orange that quenches, its bright skin encasing the natural power of sun and soil and rain. Got it.

"He always knew what I was feeling and what I was about to feel – that was the weird part. Sometimes I would cry, and it was okay. One time I felt this warm feeling building up from the back of my spine, a feeling of love that was completely impersonal. It wasn't about Dan and I. It was something about God – I don't know. It was the closest I ever came to a vaginal orgasm."

Vaginal orgasms? How did she go from reminiscing about her two years on the West Coast in the early nineties to God and the elusive vaginal orgasm? His confusion must have something to do with the monotonous two-lane country roads they're travelling, which Joseph swears are crossing and criss-crossing their way back to the train station, as if Liz brought him all the way out here to give him a quick tour of the countryside and an update on her marriage. He can't even remember how they got onto sex – the topic snuck up on them north of the station as the car passed through an area of long low hills and dips, leaking into the hyperclean car through the little window cracks the girls unrolled in the back seat. He's glad the girls disobeyed Liz, who insisted that rear windows didn't need to be opened on such a cloudy day. The wind makes a tunneling noise that confines the adult conversation to the front seats where it belongs. Franny will have plenty of time to worry about sex and God, and he's made it his life's mission as a father to defer that day of reckoning for her as long as he can.

He flips open the little mirror on the passenger-side sun visor and adjusts it until he can see Franny in the seat behind him. She is listening to Charlotte with theatrical intensity, playing the part of indulgent teacher or daycare worker to the younger girl.

"Did he ruin me, Joseph?" Liz pats him on the knee, her customary long look into his eyes unsafe in the fast traffic. "Did Dan ruin me for marriage?"

She's been doing this since they were teenagers, nailing him between the eyes with questions that demand a definitive, possibly life-altering answer, as if he possesses the power to corral and tame her anxiety with a simple yes or no. It still amazes him, her faith in questions, and he is reminded how much he admires her.

"No Liz," he tells her, "he didn't *ruin* you. He woke you up, you know, he woke up your senses to new possibilities of expression and intimacy, and you needed someone to do that at the time so that you could move on to something deeper, more long-term. Now you've got to." He is running out of words, a bad sign at so early a stage in the speech she's waiting to hear.

"Dan was like basic training." No, that's not it.

"He was like your initiator, your intimacy mentor." Christ, he sounds like a New Age guru now, all myth and symbol, but that's what she wants, for Joseph to assign Dan a place in her personal mythology so that she can fully embrace the life she's made for herself out here in the country with Mike and the kids. She wants Dan placed up on an altar in a back room, a phallic statue to be rubbed for good luck, and Joseph wants to provide this service for her but when he listens to his own heart on the matter he hears a lone voice in the wilderness crying, "Go to him Liz, give it all up – the husband, the career, the farm. Go to Dan. Track him down, Liz, wherever he's living now, and eat as many of his damn oranges as you can. Your family will be waiting when you come home."

The voice is wrong. The voice tells lies, he knows that, but there it is, petitioning his attention, distracting him from the task at hand – to help his dear old friend sign off on the troubling, glorious memories of her nights with Dan, a man still making too many surprise appearances in her dreams and fantasies.

Why is she asking this of Joseph? *Him*? He's the last person who should be giving advice on life plans and emotional moderation and taming the gods of passion, and she should know that better than almost anyone.

He checks the mirror again. Franny's taken to eavesdropping these days but according to the mirror she's still listening to one of Charlotte's rambling schoolyard epics and nodding at all the right moments. It's like Franny flips a switch when children are around. A kid sits down beside her and she turns into Mary Poppins without the umbrella or Maria from *Sound of Music* without the sing-along, all encouragement and sound advice to her young charge. But put her in a room with girls her own age, or older girls – then she's all nerves.

He studies her face in the mirror, the smooth spaces around

her mouth and eyes, hoping to catch her face in a moment of total repose. Sometimes he watches her when she's asleep. Not for very long – two minutes at most, and only when she's at his place on the weekends. When he knows she's in a deep sleep he stands in her crowded little room watching her, storing up an accumulative portrait of her face at rest. It's a neurotic habit, he knows that, an unsubtle symptom of God knows how many unresolved anxieties and hang-ups, but he needs those two minutes, just as he needs to see her face, relaxed, distracted, in the mirror above him.

"Maybe," Liz says, "maybe you can only feel that close to another person when don't have anything else going on in your life. You give your lover everything you have: every feeling, every worry, every drop of lust because there's nothing to distract you, no commitments, no kids, no career."

Let's not go there, he thinks, not here, in the car, sober with the kids all ears in the back.

"I lived only in the present," Liz tells him, "sharing everything with this one person and the smell of his skin took up as much space in my thoughts as the mortgage does now."

"I think you're right, Liz."

"I wonder."

Was this it then, the life revelation that she's been hinting at in phone calls and emails for at least the last three months – that she's going to split up with Mike while she's still young enough to find a more suitable lover, one whose passion and spontaneity and sack techniques will reawaken her deepest most authentic self. She is due for a life transformation. Twelve years with one man, and let's be honest, not a not particularly ambitious or passionate one at that. Twelve years, eight of them out here in the country, first as a social worker and overworked mother and wife, now as a budding real estate agent and even more overworked mother and wife. No wonder she'd tried so hard to persuade

Joseph to come for a visit.

He waits for her to share the revelation, preparing the encouragement and compassion she'll need from him.

He waits.

She fiddles with the radio, finding an all-talk station, and then settles back into her seat.

"What have you decided then?" he asks.

"Decided?"

Apparently he does have to spell it out. "About you and Mike?"

"Oh, nothing. What's to decide?"

He can feel himself frowning; the horizontal lines in his face pressing down on each other and getting fatter near his mouth. "I though you wanted to tell me something, before we arrived at the farm."

"Oh no." She laughs as if she's caught him trying to put one over on her. "No, Joseph, I'm just explaining to you my current state of manageable unhappiness."

He feels himself blushing. He is a total idiot sometimes. Most of the time, really.

"We watch Oprah together on Wednesdays."

"Mike?" He's only pretending to be surprised.

"Oh, he watches it ironically, or pretends to. He calls it his weekly Oprah cry."

"I'm not allowed to let on that you told me that, right?"

"Oh, I don't mind." She pauses, looks in at some memory of unselfconscious affection. "He's happier these days. He's made some friends in the community and the administrators and students like him at the college. The teaching gig pays less than the one in the city and he'll never get a permanent position, but at least he doesn't have to commute."

She is talking about Mike in an almost sisterly way, as if he's a younger brother she snuggles under the covers when the children are asleep, but Joseph knows there is more to their relationship than companionship – something deeper, more raw and vital. He's glad for her, and he plans on telling her so, maybe after they've had a few drinks tonight. He'll tell her he's happy for her and that he appreciates how she bugged him until he agreed to visit for the weekend. He needs to get out of the city more, he knows that, and it's good for him to be spending a long weekend with Franny.

The car is passing through a narrow stretch of road hemmed in on both sides by orderly rows of pine trees that whip past the window like the rotating spokes of a tire, and then suddenly they're in a village that could fit on a postcard and probably has, many times. A dozen or so stone and wood houses crowd close to the road, and there's a boxy post office across the street from a library and at the edge of the village a mill converted into a combination art gallery and cafe. They've passed a lot of these gentrified old buildings along the way, inns and mills and general stores with their original fixtures and Victorian trills replaced or replicated, their interiors stocked with antiques and local produce and art and handcrafted everything for the tourist trade.

The land opens up into another round of fields, most of which have either been harvested already or were left fallow to begin with. Liz slows down the car and points to a For Sale on the rolling lawn of what looks like a two-or three-acre hobby farm. Liz showed this place to a couple from the city yesterday, and if they buy the property it will be her tenth sale of the summer, which may not be much by other agents' standards but is great for someone who's had their real estate license for less than a year. The house is heated geothermally, she explains to Joseph, a system that costs a fortune to install but the current owners say they'd do it all over again for all the money it's saved them. Liz can really get behind this house. It's not just about helping the environment, she assures Joseph, it's about long-term savings for the client. She throws him a monthly heating-and-hydro figure and he makes a "wow" gesture, not having any idea what it normally costs to heat a place up here or anywhere else. Liz tells him that she made a promise to herself to sell the house by the end of September, and she intends to follow through.

"I guess you know who to blame if the promise is broken," he says.

"Oh, it won't be broken."

She knows he's making a joke, but she won't play along. Promises are important to her, the cornerstone of a new life philosophy that she's been learning about in a series of books and DVDs that focus on positive thinking and visualization techniques. According to the DVD, if she visualizes her goals and makes a solemn vow to keep them, those goals will be actualized over time. It's all about seeing what you want and promising yourself that you'll stay true to that vision until it comes true.

She's explained this on the phone to him a few times and each time he's chosen not to comment. She won't bring it up now. Instead she points to a Canadian Tire bill she's taped to the dashboard. The 25-cent denomination has been changed with a magic marker, so that now you could buy $250,000 worth of hardware at the chain store – if that were the point of the gesture, which it's not. Joseph knows this but he makes the joke anyways, loud enough for the girls to hear.

"You could get a lot of housewares and screws for that," he says touching the bill. He knows that Liz has been waiting for him to ask her about it because she puts her face closer to the windshield and begins talking in that tone of defensive enthusiasm that has been missing from her voice until now.

"That's how much money I've promised myself to make in the next two years," she tells him. "I wrote out that amount as a promise note to myself and a reminder of what I can do if I try hard enough. I know you think it's stupid. God, I can hear you talking to Jane about this later: *Liz's gone nuts again*."

"No, no, no," he says. He probably will say that to Jane later, but neither of them will take it literally. Saying that Liz has gone nuts again is shorthand for "Liz has found another *enthusiasm*," and the remark will be followed by what he intends as a good-natured rolling of the eyes. "I mean, it's not what I would do," he says. "But I've certainly been thinking about making money lately. I'm not afraid of it. I want money."

"Then you should make a promise to yourself to go out and get it. It's all about positive thinking," she says.

"Funny, I thought it was about getting a job with a company that pays a living wage."

She won't be swayed from her point. "I've tried negativity. Did a couple of decades of always seeing the worst in everything. That's how it was with us: we had to see the black hole in everything. We were so negative."

What decade were they talking about now? "When we were young?"

"The party years, yeah. We were so negative, so cynical."

"It was the 80s. We were reacting with eyes open."

"It was more than that. It wasn't cool to be optimistic."

"It wasn't cool to be *naive*," he corrects her. He doesn't want to defend how things were when they were younger, but the habit of taking her hand in an argument like she's his little sister at a crosswalk is still deeply ingrained. He knows he's doing it and he knows it's wrong but to suddenly stop acting according to precedent would be – what? Exhausting, probably. He's already tired. Being in a car makes him sleepy. So he'll act in character. It doesn't matter – it's not like he's hurting her. She even told him the last time he visited that she was glad that he'd been so hard on her back in the day, and that if he hadn't punished her for her naivety and set her straight about the cold hard world that she probably would have ended up dead or in a cult. It's hard for him to think about those times and imagine himself helping anybody. Joseph helping Liz, doing something for her benefit alone – he must have been drunk, transported by one of those rapturous hazes of generalized love that nailed him near the end of a three-night bender, like his own version of Sunday penitence. But it's a nice thought, that underneath all that posturing and womanizing and glory chasing there was a better, finer self watching over his friends as they rode out their own dramas. He imagines this finer self as a quiet, priestly-looking man drained of the sex need, with a broad high forehead and the kind of eyes that frighten Joseph, watery irises made sharper, bluer by the moisture. He'd like to meet this fine man and hear his version of those mythic days of yore, ask him what really went down and who did what to whom.

Dani Couture

SHRIMPING: A POSTCARD

picture came

yesterday, slipped as bait
into the open mouth

of my mailbox. the soft, fingered edges
of foreign stationery, his signature

lines & expressions unfurled
like cold st. lawrence currents

over my continental body.
he is shrimping now, baiting hooks:

a warm cement pool gouged
into taichung's already choked lungs.

caught white and heavy-handed
in between a day-glo green rice patty

& a dan bing stand. fisting a can
of acidic chinese brew, he chats with locals.

he, in search of anything. western
hunger waning into a simple desire –

the capture of a creature
only capable of swimming backwards,

away.

THE ENDS

on parting, i give you ends –
the final moments of things accumulated.

the street, with its last breath. a stop.
a lone sign to make you yield. *if only.*

moments teetering on the crisp edge of shirttails,
street-worn soles moving steadily away.

somewhere, the last pages of every novel bound
together – a convergence of loose ends tied for you.

a barrel full with apple cores – seeds
like soft black pearls pressed into amber flesh.

by thumbs – the ends of my hands – i give you
every conceivable end to fall from.

even the ends of sentences cut short. stumble over
implication into the next. i give you winter.

Stacey May Fowles

UNCONVINCING

MARNIE ALWAYS WANTED to be an outreach worker for drug-addled street youth, but instead she works as a perfume counter girl at a major downtown department store on evenings and weekends. This is partly due to the fact that Marnie's mother told her she didn't have the stomach to be an outreach worker for the drug-addled, and that Marnie's boyfriend discouraged her from studying to become an outreach worker because there was a need for immediate income in the face of his doing a PhD in comparative literature.

Marnie owns three knee-length black skirts, each one purchased at the same mall in the same store for $19.99. Each skirt is a slightly different style and a uniform requirement of her job as a perfume counter girl. On the way to work each day she drops yesterday's black knee-length skirt at the dry cleaner in the same mall where she works. The elderly male attendant who is always behind the counter and who she assumes is the owner takes the skirt from her hands and stares straight through her, telling her the cost daily through his nicotine-stained beard despite the fact that she has the cost memorized and therefore always has exact change ready. The first few months she worked at the perfume counter she waited for the old man in the dry cleaner to recognize her, acknowledge her return on one of her many skirt drop-offs, participate in some witty banter, but he never did and Marnie gave up on expecting him to do so.

The dry cleaner's lack of witty banter injustice is directly responsible for Marnie's complete and total debilitating fear that she will become like the woman behind the counter at her local Hasty Mart. As the woman packs up Marnie's six eggs and three tins of cat food something in her face seems to suggest she has endured a lifetime of being stared through.

Marnie doesn't know that the dry cleaner has Alzheimer's that will be discovered by his doctor two weeks after they pull her boyfriend's body from the lake.

Marnie will be thirty soon.

After her shift at the perfume counter and after making her purchases at the Hasty Mart, Marnie goes home to the tiny apartment she shares with her boyfriend who is doing his PhD in comparative literature and Marnie stares into the bathroom mirror without unpacking the six eggs and three tins of cat food. She is looking for evidence that she does indeed exist, that despite the fact that no one connects with her at any moment during the day she is still flesh and bone. She squeezes her cheek just to be sure as the cat curls around her feet on the fraying blue bathmat. The squeeze leaves a mark of vibrant pink and then the flash fades suddenly into nothing. The cat looks up and meows to be fed. She forgets to unpack the eggs and put them in the fridge before she goes to bed and therefore throws them into the garbage the following morning.

Marnie's boyfriend, who is doing his PhD in comparative literature, hasn't been home in five days.

During the day Marnie wakes around noon, and eats a poached egg on rye toast while she reads the books she buys on the Internet. Daily they arrive in her mailbox from all over the world, first editions, new releases and rare signed copies, each one read and then carefully placed in alphabetical order in milk crates in the hall closet. Aside from the books, the hall closet also has hundreds of coat hangers in it, each one from the dry cleaner in the mall, given to her by a man who will never recognize her despite the fact that she is there almost daily.

At three in the afternoon Marnie showers and slips into a

freshly dry cleaned black skirt, and depending on the day it is slim fitting, A-line or pleated. The pleated skirt costs more to be dry cleaned. Marnie feeds the cat and checks the mail and takes the subway to the mall. While she is on the subway she notices a rather large, muscular man in a beer T-shirt with a shaved head and the name Carol tattooed all over his body. The name is written in grand looping letters up his left calve, contained in a bursting bleeding red heart on his right forearm, and scripted small in the bulldog folds in the back of his neck.

Marnie is sure that Carol's beauty is convincing.

Marnie's boyfriend, who is doing his PhD in comparative literature, hasn't been home in six days.

Marnie tries her best to look pretty at the perfume counter, but she doesn't really understand why she was hired for a job that's success is dependant on how convincing her beauty is. Marnie believes it to be unconvincing. She believes that her boyfriend has left her for one of the undergraduate students in a class he TA's for, believes that the undergraduate's beauty is probably convincing, that the drycleaner would see her and that she would never fear, would never become the woman behind the counter at the Hasty Mart. Marnie believes it is the undergraduate's phone number she found in the pocket of her boyfriend's gray overcoat when she took it to be dry cleaned and was not acknowledged by the man who works behind the counter. Marnie also believes the undergraduate student is the reason she discovered she had Chlamydia at her last doctor's appointment.

Marnie likes to leave messages without making phone calls, never having to return inquiries directly, merely pressing a button and recording a response onto someone's voice mail. She enjoys the lack of intimacy that technology affords her.

Marnie cannot recall a time in her life where she has been satisfied, although she additionally cannot recall a time in her life where she has actually complained to anyone about being dissatisfied.

Marnie's boyfriend is bloated and blue, a heavy drinker who drove into the lake and now lays there motionless as the waves lap the shore and his flesh pulls and pops away from bone. The fish gnaw at his pockmarked skin as Marnie daydreams of him making love to her, daydreams of him making love to a petite blonde undergraduate student whose phone number she found in his grey overcoat pocket.

Marnie's boyfriend did his PhD in comparative literature simply because at dinner and cocktail parties it seemed more appropriate to announce academia as his vocation rather than "telemarketer." He hasn't been home in seven days.

On this, the seventh day, Marnie's mother calls long distance from their family home on the west coast while Marnie is poaching an egg and watching the cat chase imaginary spiders across the living room rug.

"Marianne," she says in her raspy pack-a-day voice, "you should really get out more. Make some new friends. Go out with the girls in the cosmetics department."

"I know."

"How's Michael?"

Michael is doing his PhD in comparative literature and hasn't been home in seven days. A petite blonde undergraduate student is calling his cell phone and getting his voice mail. The petite blonde undergraduate student is assuming Michael has decided not to leave his frumpy girlfriend and as a result she is now plotting martinis with her girlfriends and make out sessions with strangers. Michael is at the bottom of a lake in the driver's seat of an '84 Volvo being eaten by fish.

"He's fine."

Marnie and Michael have been together for three years. Michael wanted Marnie to be on the pill despite the fact that it made her gain sixteen pounds and her moods unbearable. She had to buy three brand new knee-length black skirts because she went up two waist sizes. Since she went off the pill without telling Michael, she has gone up yet another waist size. She has an appointment at the Women's clinic on Friday, which will be the ninth day Michael has failed to come home and the sixteenth day Marnie has been late.

Marnie has never had an orgasm.

On the eighth day the petite undergraduate student unexpectedly arrives at Marnie's front door at two in the afternoon. She is wearing an emerald green mini-dress and a pair of patent leather kitten heels. As predicted, she is convincingly pretty, and apparently drunk.

"Where's Michael?" she asks without introducing herself.

"At the university," Marnie replies deadpan.

"You're a fucking liar."

"You gave me Chlamydia."

Marnie slams the door in the pretty blonde's face and goes back to getting ready for her shift at the perfume counter. She can hear the undergraduate student call her an "ugly cunt" from the other side of the door as she unsheathes a black skirt from its gauzy plastic casing and slips a second black skirt into her backpack.

"That'll be $4.36," the dry cleaner says.

"I know," Marnie replies.

Marnie is almost thirty.

On the ninth day Marnie has a conversation with a plump and pleasant woman at the clinic about "options" and comes home to find that the cat has killed a grey mouse and left it for her on the bathroom floor. There are three messages on the answering machine. The first is from the University stating that Michael has not attended a week of tutorials, the second from Michael's mother wondering where he is, the third a series of curse words from the petite blonde undergraduate student.

Marnie unplugs the phone.

When the police arrive on the tenth day, her day off and a Sunday, Marnie is picking out baby names and writing them in neat gendered columns in a small steno pad. She makes them a pot of coffee and answers all of their questions politely.

"I last saw him on a Thursday. We had lunch."

"He was wearing a torn black sweater and blue jeans."

"No. He didn't seem distressed or out of sorts."

"We have been together or three years."

"I miss him."

"I didn't report it because I assumed he had left me for one of his students."

Things Marnie didn't say included:

"I didn't care that he had left me."

"The day we had lunch I told him I was late and he had too many gin and tonics and as a result called me a miserable bitch."

"He was suffocating me with his narcissism."

"I am carrying his child because I was deceptive. I am picking out names and writing them in neat gendered columns in this steno pad that is lying between us on the kitchen table. I don't want him to be involved. In fact, if he is dead I would feel a sense of morbid relief because I despise my life and have allowed him to become the architect of it."

Michael is no longer the architect of Marnie's despised life. Michael is at the bottom of a lake in the driver's seat of an '84 Volvo being eaten by fish and receiving angry, pleading voice mail messages from a blonde undergraduate student.

On the twelfth day they pull the '84 Volvo and Michael's blue and bloated body out from the bottom of the lake. Marnie receives a message stating that she is required to come and identify the body, a body that is wearing a torn black sweater and blue jeans. On the way home from the morgue she buys six eggs and three tins of cat food from the Hasty Mart.

It is discovered that the owner of the dry cleaner has Alzheimer's and his thirty-eight year old daughter who has never married (and likes it that way) temporarily replaces him behind the counter.

Marnie's list of baby names, neatly written in a steno pad on the kitchen table, exceeds one hundred possible choices. During the week that Michael's body has been found she has been busy transcribing them into a separate list, this one in alphabetical order.

The following week when she returns to work she drops off a black knee-length skirt at the dry cleaner and pays $4.36 in exact change.

"You must come here often," the dry cleaner's daughter says.

Marnie is thirty.

Karen Solie

PATHOLOGY OF THE SENSES

Oligotrophic: of lakes and rivers. The heat
an inanimate slur, a wool gathering, hanging
like a bad suit. Suspended fine particulate

matter. And an eight-million-dollar ferry shoves off
for Rochester with no souls aboard. I see you,
you know, idling like a limousine through the old

neighbourhoods, your tinted windows. In what
they call "the mind's eye." Catch me here
in real time, if that's the term for it. We're working

our drinks under threat of a general brownout.
Phospholipase: bitter stimuli activate it.
Back home, we call this a beer parlour.

I washed my hair at 4 a.m., he says. *The full moon,
it was whack.* He can't sleep. The woman
who says *pardon my French*, over and over,

can't sleep. They are drunk as young corn. Sweet,
white, freestone peaches. A bit stepped-on.
You said we'd have fun. Do I look happy?

Our fingers, our ankles, swelling in unison. Word
spreads quickly. "Toronto," in Huron, means
"place of meetings." Even now, you may be

darkening my door. *On my bike*, she says, *I dress
all reflective*. Even now, you're troubling
my windbreak. The vertebrate heart muscle

does not fatigue and is under the regulation
of nerves. I'll wait. First it is unlike evening.
Then it is unlike night. Thirty degrees in a false

high noon, no shade to be found when all things
lie in shadow. The lake is a larger mind
with pressures brought to bear, a wet hot headache

in the hind brain. Above it, cloud racks up.
A mean idea it's taking to, breathing
through its mouth. In this year of Our Lord

your approach shoulders in like the onset
of a chronic understanding. There are rivers
underfoot, paved over. The Humber, Taddle Creek.

Just the way they sound. To be abyssal
is to inhabit deep water roughly below 1,000 feet.
I need a good costume, he says, *but don't know*

what that entails. Walk the districts. There,
the misery of historic buildings. Here,
the superheated rooms of the poor. Sorry,

cooling station closed. Lack of funding. I like
my feet covered up at night, doesn't everyone.
Blinking, we lie naked atop our sheets.

Spare a dollar for a half-hour in an air-conditioned
cyber-cafe? Okay. Now get lost. My mood
this day is palpable and uncertain. Our smoke

rises but does not disperse. The air hairy as a fly.
In fly weather. Tight under the arms.
It also depletes your spinal fluid. In your spine.

The aesthetic injury level is the degree
of pest abundance above which control measures
should be taken. God, what she's wearing.

I'm tolerably certain you know the way. The red
tide of the sidewalks. Pass the dry cleaners
and *Wigs, Wigs, Wigs!* It used to be called

100% Human Hair! That's right. "Ontario"
is an Iroquois word meaning "sparkling waters."
Like doleful seaweed, our predilections undulate.

Rats come out to sniff the garbage blooms
in rat weather. Heavy cloud the colour of slag
and tailings, a green light gathering inside

like an angry jelly. Pardon my French. And the city
on its rails, grinding toward a wreck the lake
cooks up. Its lake effect. When you arrive you may

be soaked to the skin. A tall drink of water. Darken
my door. *All of my organs are fully involved.*
He is a little freshet breeze. We are as any microbes

inhabiting an extreme environment, surviving
in the free-living or parasitic mode. Chins above
the germ line. Is it true a rat can spring a latch.

Is it true all creatures love their children. Raccoons
and skunks smell society in decline. That sag
at the middle. In rat weather. Fly weather. A certain

absence of tenderness. Who will you believe.
Bear me away to a motel by the highway. I like
a nice motel by the highway. An in-ground pool.

It's a take it or leave it type deal. Eutrophic: of lakes
and rivers. *See now*, she says, *that's the whole reason
you can't sit up on the railing. So you don't*

fall over. Freon, exhaust, the iron motes of a dry
lightning. *Getting pushed*, he says, *is not
falling*. Jangling metal in your pockets

you walk balanced in your noise, breath
like a beam. I harbour ill will in my heart.
By this shall you know me. Caducous:

not persistent. Of sepals, falling off
as a flower opens. Of stipules, falling off as leaves
unfold. Speak of the devil and the devil appears.

IV
LOUNGE NIGHTS

Contributors

MICHAEL BRYSON is the author of two short story collections: *Thirteen Shades of Black and White* and *Only a Lower Paradise*. He is also the founding editor and publisher of the online literary magazine *The Danforth Review*. His story "Six Million Million Miles" appeared in *05: Best Canadian Stories* (Oberon Press, 2005).

EVIE CHRISTIE lives in Toronto. She is the author of *Gutted* (ECW Press) and more recently her work appeared in the anthology *Jailbreaks: 99 Canadian Sonnets* (Biblioasis Press).

DAVID LIVINGSTONE CLINK is a poet who has never owned a dog, or served in the military. He is the Artistic Director of the Rowers Pub Reading Series, and likes eating fruit out of season. His first book-length collection, *Eating Fruit out of Season*, will be published by Tightrope Books in 2008. He likes puns. And surrealism. And sushi. You can find him at poetrymachine.com.

DANI COUTURE published *Good Meat* with Pedlar Press in 2006 and is currently working on a second collection of poetry, *The Handbook*. Her work has been published in journals and magazines across Canada, including the Globe and Mail, *Taddle Creek*, *The Fiddlehead*, *Arc* and *This Magazine*. "shrimping: a postcard," and "the ends" appeared in *Good Meat*.

ANDREW DALEY works in the film and television business. His first novel, *Tell Your Sister*, was published in June of 2007. He is also the associate editor of *Taddle Creek*.

STACEY MAY FOWLES has had work published in various online and print magazines, including *Kiss Machine*, *Girlistic*, *The Absinthe Literary Review*, *Hive* and *subTERRAIN*. Her non-fiction has been anthologized in the widely acclaimed *Nobody Passes: Rejecting the Rules of Gender and Conformity* and *First Person Queer*. Her first novel, *Be Good*, was published in 2007. She is the publisher of *Shameless Magazine*.

CATHERINE GRAHAM is the author of *The Watch*, *Pupa* and *The Red Element*. She teaches creative writing at the University of Toronto, designs and delivers workshops on creativity for the business and academic communities, and is Vice President of Project Bookmark Canada. "Heavy Without Heavy Rain," appeared in *Taddle Creek*.

JAMES GRAINGER is a books columnist for the Toronto Star and Quill & Quire and the author of *The Long Slide* (ECW Press), which won the ReLit Award for short fiction in 2005. He is currently finishing work on two novels, including *All This, in Front of the Children*, which he will be pitching to publishers as "a cross between The Big Chill and Deliverance." He has always lived in Toronto.

RAY HSU is author of an award-winning book of poems, Anthropy. He has published poems in *The Walrus*, *New American Writing*, and *Fence*. He is a doctoral candidate at the University of Wisconsin-Madison where he also teaches in a nearby prison.

LEIGH KOTSILIDIS is a poet, installation artist and stop-animator, who also dabbles in music. Her poetry has appeared in anthologies, chapbook form, and in Canadian journals. In 2007 she attended the Banff Writing Studio where she made some headway on her poetry manuscript *Hypotheticals*. She recently relocated to Montreal.

KATHRYN KUITENBROUWER has a novel forthcoming in the spring of 2009. Her novel *The Nettle Spinner* was nominated for the Amazon. ca/Books in Canada First Novel Award. Her story collection, *Way Up*, won a Danuta Gleed Award and was shortlisted for the ReLit Award. She lives in Toronto.

ALEXANDRA LEGGAT writes fiction and poetry and instructs creative writing classes. Her work has been published across Canada and the U.S. and her books can be found in bookshops near you. "Kid Airplane" is part of her newest short story collection.

SHARON MCCARTNEY is the author of *Against* (Frog Hollow Press, 2007), *The Love Song of Laura Ingalls Wilder* (Nightwood Editions, 2007), *Switchgrass Stills* (littlefishcartpress, 2006), *Karenin Sings the Blues* (Goose Lane Editions, 2003) and *Under the Abdominal*

Wall (Anvil Press, 1999). Her poems have been frequently selected as finalists in Arc's Poem of the Year contest. "Coyote" appeared in *Against*, and "Dorothy," in *Arc*. "Against Coyotes" appeared in the chapbook *Against*.

STEVE MCORMOND's first book of poetry, *Lean Days*, was short listed for the 2005 Gerald Lampert Award. His second collection, *Primer on the Hereafter*, was awarded the 2007 Atlantic Poetry Prize. His work also appears in the anthology *Breathing Fire 2: Canada's New Poets*. He lives in Toronto. "The End of the World" first appeared in *Arc 57* (Winter 2006) and "Donut Shop" first appeared in *Event 32.1* (2003).

ALAYNA MUNCE grew up in Huntsville, Ontario, and now lives in Toronto. In 2003 she won a prize in the CBC Literary Awards, and in 2004 her work was selected for the anthology *Breathing Fire 2: Canada's New Poets*. Her first novel, *When I Was Young and In My Prime* (Nightwood Editions, 2005) has appeared on the national bestseller list for Canadian fiction and was nominated for a Trillium Book Award.

MOLLY PEACOCK is poetry editor of the Literary Review of Canada and General Series Editor of *The Best Canadian Poetry in English* as well as the author of six volumes of poetry, including *The Second Blush*, forthcoming from W.W. Norton and Company. Her poems have appeared in *The Best of the Best American Poetry* and *The Oxford Book of American Poetry*.

EMILY SCHULTZ wrote a collection of short fiction, *Black Coffee Night*, shortlisted for the Danuta Gleed Award, as well as a novel called *Joyland*, and a collection of poems, *Songs for the Dancing Chicken*. Her upcoming novel will be called *Heaven Is Small*. "I Love You, Pretty Puppy" is a story that appeared in *Taddle Creek*.

SUE SINCLAIR's latest collection of poems, *Breaker*, will be published by Brick Books in the fall of 2008. Sue is currently living in Toronto where she is studying philosophy.

GORAN SIMIC is recognized in Europe and the US for his works of poetry, fiction, essays and theatrical drama. He has been translated into nine languages as well as published in various countries. His books published in Canada so far include the poetry books *Immigrant Blues* and *From Sarajevo With Sorrow*, and the fiction collection *Yesterday's People*.

MICHAEL V SMITH is a Vancouver writer, filmmaker, comedian, performance artist and occasional clown. Smith's novel, *Cumberland* (Cormorant Books, 2002), was nominated for the Amazon/Books in Canada First Novel Award. His latest book is *What You Can't Have* (Signature Editions, 2006), a collection of poetry, was shortlisted for the ReLit Prize.

SHAUN SMITH is a writer, journalist and editor from Toronto whose work has appeared in *Toronto Life*, *Quill & Quire*, *The Toronto Star* and elsewhere. His novel *Snakes & Ladders* is forthcoming in 2009 from The Dundurn Group.

KAREN SOLIE won the Dorothy Livesay Poetry Prize and was shortlisted for a number of other prizes for her first collection of poems, *Short Haul Engine*. Her second, *Modern and Normal*, was shortlisted for a Trillium Award and included on the *Globe and Mail*'s list of the 100 best books of 2005. "Pathology" appeared in a 2006 issue of *Brick*.

CARMINE STARNINO has published three books of poetry, for which he has won the Canadian Authors Associate Prize, the A.M. Klein Prize and the F.G. Bressani Prize. He was recently included in *Best American Poetry 2007*. He lives in a Montreal.

MOEZ SURANI has poetry and short fiction that has appeared in journals and anthologies in Europe and North America. He has won the Kingston Literary Award, the *Dublin Quarterly*'s Poem of the Year, and most recently was on the shortlist for the 2007 CBC Literary Award. His debut collection of poems, *Reticent Bodies*, is forthcoming from Wolsak & Wynn.

MATTHEW TIERNEY lives in Toronto. His first poetry collection is *Full Speed through the Morning Dark*, from Wolsak & Wynn. A second manuscript won the K.M. Hunter Award for Literature. *Seven Phobias*, a 'chipbook' published by littlefishcartpress, does not include "Parelasiphobia." "Optic Nerve" was previously published in *THIS Magazine*.

MATTHEW J TRAFFORD has published poems, stories, and reviews in journals across Canada, including *The Malahat Review, Books in Canada, The Dalhousie Review, echolocation,* and *The Dominion*. Many thanks to Alex Boyd for the invitation to read in the series (March 23rd, 2007) and to submit to the anthology.

JESSICA WESTHEAD is a Toronto writer who has published stories in litmags such as *The Antigonish Review, Matrix, THIS Magazine, Geist, Taddle Creek,* and *Kiss Machine*. Her short story chapbook, *Those Girls*, was published by Greenboathouse Books in 2006, and her first novel, *Pulpy and Midge*, was published by Coach House Books in fall 2007. The I.V. Lounge is one of her favourite places to read, and she has been vocalizing her tales there since 2001. "Gar's Marine Palace" first appeared in *Forget Magazine*.

ROB WINGER lives in Ottawa with his family and is the author of *Muybridge's Horse*, shortlisted for the 2007 Governor General's Award for poetry.

HEATHER J WOOD lives in Toronto with her poetic husband and two feline pets. Her fiction has appeared in *Kiss Machine, Artistry of Life, Litbits,* the anthology *In the Dark* and in the Press On! chapbook, *Barbies, Breasts and Bathing Suits*.

Editors

ALEX BOYD was born in Toronto. He writes poems, fiction, reviews and essays, and has had work published in magazines and newspapers such as *Taddle Creek*, *Books in Canada*, *The Globe and Mail*, *Quill & Quire*, *The Antigonish Review* and on various websites such as *The Danforth Review*, *Nthposition*, and *PoetryX*. In Toronto he is the organizer and host of the I.V. Lounge Reading Series, and he is the co-editor of Northern Poetry Review, an online home for poetry reviews, essays and articles. His personal site is alexboyd.com. His first book of poems, *Making Bones Walk*, was published in 2007 by Luna Publications.

MYNA WALLIN is a poet, prose writer, editor, and radio host. She's also a team member of the Art Bar Reading Series. Myna's first full-length collection of poetry, *A Thousand Profane Pieces*, was published by Tightrope Books in June 2006. Starting January 2007, she took on the position of Poetry Editor at Tightrope and has edited Sandra Kasturi's *The Animal Bridegroom* (2007), co-edited (with Halli Villegas) *The Stone Skippers* by Ian Burgham (2007) and the anthology, *In the Dark: Stories from the Supernatural* (2006). Myna also hosts "In Other Words" on CKLN and she's working on a novella entitled *Confessions of a Reluctant Cougar*. Her personal site is mynawallin.com.

She'd like to add that it was a pleasure working on this anthology with the multi-talented, decisive and always mellow, Alex Boyd. Thanks to Halli for her faith in this project, her consummate artistic vision, and her friendship.